SANDRA LEE
MADE FROM SCRATCH

ALSO BY SANDRA LEE

SANDRA LEE
MADE FROM SCRATCH

A Memoir

Meredith® Books   Des Moines, Iowa

Meredith Books
1716 Locust Street
Des Moines, Iowa 50309-3023
meredithbooks.com

Cover and page 6 photographs: Melanie Dunea

First Edition. Printed in the United States of America.
Library of Congress Control Number: 2007936356
ISBN: 978-0-696-23919-9

It takes courage to grow up and turn out to be who you really are.

E. E. Cummings

CONTENTS

The person who moves a mountain begins by carrying away small stones.

anonymous

DEDICATION

This book is dedicated to everyone who has faced challenges in life and questioned the purpose of hard times. Everything happens for a reason, and you are not alone. I hope my story inspires you to endure the rough days and enjoy the easier ones. Know in your heart that anything is possible if you work hard and wish it so.

Chapter One
To Grandma's House We Go

So if you have a grandma, thank the good Lord above, and give grandmamma hugs and kisses, for grandmothers are to love.

Lois Wyse
Grandmothers Are to Love

I was about 2 years old when my mother, Vicky, dropped my younger sister, Cindy, and me off at Grandma Lorraine's house in Santa Monica one beautiful sunny afternoon in 1968.

She left that day promising to return shortly. We didn't see her again for several years.

I don't remember ever hearing any rational explanations or even any conversations about Vicky's absence, but I do recall wondering where she was. Grandma rarely talked to us about our missing mother. I don't think she quite knew what to say, and I'm sure she didn't want to lie to me. Vicky was just 18 years old when she left and probably couldn't handle the responsibility of raising us.

Grandma Lorraine was the mother of my birth father, Wayne. Vicky and Wayne were typical high school sweethearts—young, naive, and head over heels in love. When Vicky became pregnant with me at 15, she and Wayne decided to get married at the Santa Monica courthouse. Vicky's parents were less than enthusiastic about the decision but they were staunch Catholics and even though Vicky and Wayne were just children themselves, any other decision would have been unacceptable. I don't think it came as a surprise to anyone that they weren't able to make their relationship work. They filed for divorce about two years after they said, "I do," and somewhere around Cindy's first birthday. Although I don't remember it, Wayne often came to Grandma's house to visit.

Shortly after Vicky dropped Cindy and me off at Grandma's, two of Wayne's and Vicky's friends from high school, Doug, and Doug's older brother, Richard, went into the military. Doug was sent to serve in Vietnam.

Richard returned home sad and exhausted from his military service, mourning the loss of Doug, who had died when a mortar hit his foxhole. Somehow he reconnected with Vicky, who had always been fun loving, free-spirited, and sweet, and though they had never been romantically involved before, they started dating and married soon after. They both needed a secure foundation and found it in one another.

Of course I didn't know or understand any of this; I was too young. What I did know was that I was a happy child, living with my grandmother in a warm, carefree, and loving home. By the time I started talking, I was calling Grandma Lorraine "Mommy." She was the only mother I had ever known. Vicky was a distant memory.

Grandma Lorraine had milky white skin, kind brown eyes, and dark wavy hair. She wore pretty 1950s dresses and cashmere cardigans. Grandma was 5 feet 2 inches tall and always wore sensible, comfortable flat shoes. When I was a little girl, I thought she looked exactly like Snow White. I wanted to be just like her when I grew up. I wanted to cut my hair short like hers, to wear beautiful full-skirted dresses, and to present myself as gracefully as she did.

Grandma Lorraine loved being in the kitchen. To her it was the center of our home and a place to be enjoyed. Some of my fondest memories are of baking with Grandma in the kitchen in her cottage on Grant Street, which was just a few blocks from the Pacific Ocean. She made the most fantastic cakes. Her buttercream frosting and vanilla cake was my favorite. My birthday and Cindy's are only four days apart, and every year Grandma baked each of us our own special cake.

With a flip of her wrist, she turned two ordinary disposable aluminum pie shells into grand, shiny silver cake pedestals. On the top of each, she placed a single 8-inch cake, which she iced in white frosting, giving her a perfect canvas for dozens of bright pink flowers and rich green leaves. Her cakes came to life like her beautiful hydrangea bushes in our yard. Grandma was a masterful cake decorator with the precision of an artist. But the truth is she could have slathered icing on anything and I would have loved it.

Her baking was renowned at church bake sales. Members of the congregation asked Grandma to bake cakes for their special occasions. Weddings, birthdays, and bridal and baby showers were her favorites. She never allowed anyone to pay for the cakes. These were her gifts, her way to give them something special that meant more than money. My memories of Grandma Lorraine baking are among my most precious. Every time I use her recipe, I still feel that same special sense that I did as a child.

Grandma Lorraine was a modest woman who didn't have much money. She worked as a cafeteria food server near our home. She and Grandpa Al split long before Cindy and I arrived, though they never divorced.

Grandpa Al was a professional housepainter who helped Grandma financially even after they separated and he was particularly generous when it came to Cindy and me. Grandma Lorraine knew how to stretch a dollar better than anyone, mostly because she had to. She taught me to save money at an early age, helping me to open my very own savings account when I was 4. Grandma showed me how to fill in the registry of the blue savings book and how to fill out deposit slips too. Grandma made savings fun. I could barely spell my own name, but filling in the dollar amount on the deposit slips was easy for me. These were important lessons that would come in very handy years later.

Grandma Lorraine loved talking about tomorrow. She reminded us what a gift life was and how important it was to embrace the joy in each and every day. She spoke about all of the possibilities that tomorrow could bring. She energetically shared her enthusiasm, which made something as simple as going to the grocery store come to life like a great adventure. She talked about what the cookies would look like in the bakery, which parking spot the angels would save for us, and her never-ending quest to find the perfect peaches for her pie. She was caring, loving, and nurturing—everything a mommy should be to little girls.

Grandma was also the queen of clipping coupons. She made a family event out of cutting them from our daily newspaper and the special Sunday supplements so she could maximize the double and even triple value on certain days. We'd go off to the grocery store, coupons in hand, and there were days I thought the store would have to give us back money! Her frugality taught us to be thoughtful about finances and to understand the value of money.

Cindy always sat in the front of the cart because she was the baby, and I got to stand in the basket because I was the "big" girl. Grandma navigated her way up and down the aisles in search of the best bargains and biggest savings. She taught me which foods were pantry staples, which ones were there for pure comfort, and how to combine the two to make the ordinary extraordinary. She always allowed us to pick one special item for ourselves. I usually wanted that little red box of raisins. I loved fishing out a golden plump sweet treat with my tiny fingers. Because we were allowed one special treat, Grandma taught us to choose wisely.

Another great adventure with Grandma were our trips to the Salvation Army store. As a child I never owned a stitch of clothing that wasn't secondhand. Grandma made it an event to find the world's greatest treasures buried in the boxes lined up on the floor and on top of the shelves against the back cinder block walls of the store. We always found fantastic deals so we could buy more with our money.

She loved to buy us "princess dresses," old 1940s and '50s evening gowns made of satin and tulle, which were ideal dress-up clothes for my sister and me. After we selected our dresses, we got to rummage through the costume jewelry and accessories, picking out all of the ornate and glamorous things we needed to complete our outfits.

Our "dress-up" days were the best days of all. Grandma let us play with lipstick and paint our fingernails and toes. While we were playing, Grandma would thoughtfully lay out our pretty matching outfits to wear the next day. She dressed us in short white socks with lace around the top, which matched our patent leather Mary Jane shoes.

Dinner was between five and six in the evening. The meals I shared with Grandma growing up weren't fancy, but they were always special. When I asked her why the meals were so yummy, she told me that love was her secret ingredient. After dinner Grandma allowed us to have an hour of party time during which she turned on our favorite Alvin and the Chipmunks record. Cindy and I would dance and sing along with the songs as loudly as we could. As we settled for the evening, Grandma read us bedtime stories and scripture every night before we went to sleep.

Saturday nights were extra special. My grandma's sister-in-law and best friend, Aunt Betty, always came over for a wonderful evening spent listening to big band records, watching Lawrence Welk, and eating warm toasted strawberry Pop-Tarts, one of my absolute favorite treats. We were allowed to stay up an extra hour and sleep with her in the big bed, Cindy on one side of Grandma and me on the other. We'd fall asleep listening to Bible stories that aired on the transistor radio.

When Grandma had to go to work, Aunt Betty often took care of Cindy and me. Grandma and Aunt Betty both supported us and I don't think they could have done it without one another. My sister and I were very happy to be the center of both their lives. During the days, Aunt Betty loved to cut patterns and sew matching flowered Hawaiian dresses for us. Grandma and Aunt Betty treated us as if we were twins, equal in every way.

Aunt Betty worked as a waitress at the Santa Monica airport diner. She used her tip money to give us the special things that we couldn't always afford. Whenever we went to visit, we always sat at the counter on the pink swivel stools that matched her pink uniform and nurse-style hat. She made the most delicious ice cream sundaes with fresh strawberries, an extra dollop of whipped cream, and a huge cherry on top. Sometimes she would even have enough extra money to surprise us with a special trip to Disneyland. My sister and I loved to spin on the teacup ride until we got so dizzy that it made Grandma sick!

On the day of my sixth birthday, I skipped up to Grandpa Al's house as I usually did on a special occasion. He always gave me five silver dollars for my birthday. But this year I was turning 6. It was a big year, so I knew that I would receive six silver coins, representing the same dollar amount as my age. But Grandpa handed me the usual—five shiny silver dollars.

I put my hand on my hip and said, "Grandpa. I'm 6 years old now. You only gave me five dollars!"

Didn't he know I was 6? Hadn't grandma told him?

Grandpa Al was a little shocked at first. He looked at Grandma and then back at me. Beaming, he handed over one more silver dollar and then turned to Grandma Lorraine and said, "Yup. She's ours!"

We had a good laugh over my sassiness. But hey, a silver dollar is a silver dollar! Even I knew that!

In Vicky's absence Grandma Lorraine and Aunt Betty had raised us for about three years as their own little girls. I was never fully aware of all the sacrifices they must have made to provide such a wonderful home for my sister and me. They made it seem easy even though it must have been very hard. We were their dolls to be played with, coddled, and cherished.

Often Grandma sat me in her lap as she stroked my hair, talking face-to-face about anything and everything I was curious about and she wanted to share. Cindy would always crawl up onto the couch, hoisting one leg over and in between Grandma and me, plopping herself right down in the middle, giggling all the time as if she had done something naughty. Grandma and I were thrilled to have her. She was the baby and needed more attention than I did. We took great pride and joy in including Cindy in our one-on-one time. She was the center of our affection. Without any words Grandma could look me in the eye and convey to me that I was the big sister and I was to take care of Cindy.

Religion, education, and structure were extremely important in our home. Grandma was a very religious woman who devoted herself to helping others and giving back to the community. She was a Seventh-day Adventist and every Saturday we attended Sabbath school, where we learned about the Bible and the stories of Jesus. Many of the lessons were taught through arts and crafts projects. I made bookmarks using biblical characters and paperweights from rocks, felt, and Magic Markers, which made perfect Mother's Day gifts. Sabbath school was the birthplace of my interest in crafting, and Mother's Day was the perfect opportunity to create Grandma's favorite gifts. Who would ever have thought that I'd someday grow up and make a living at it!

Holidays were also fun and festive at home. Grandma Lorraine decorated every nook and cranny. Christmas, Easter, and birthdays were the most joyous occasions. Cindy and I made cards by hand, finger paintings, homemade decorations, and one-of-a-kind presents. Grandma Lorraine taught us to stretch our imaginations and be creative by using common household items to make our art. We used old discarded buttons, Popsicle sticks, pipe cleaners, fabric remnants, and recycled greeting cards that weren't saved in our scrapbooks.

I don't recall Grandma Lorraine ever being a strict disciplinarian, but I do remember terribly upsetting her one day at church after Sabbath school. On Saturdays, Cindy and I often helped Grandma Lorraine put together the weekly offering. We'd help her pour the grape juice that represented wine and spread out an entire box of Wheat Thins that represented the Host, which the minister used for the service.

One afternoon, Cindy and I snuck off and ate the crackers underneath the skirted table where Grandma Lorraine set up her goodies. Wheat Thins were another favorite snack and we polished off the entire box before Grandma noticed. That was a bad idea. It was the only time I ever saw Grandma angry or can remember her scolding us. We were in huge trouble, and she barely spoke to us for the rest of the day. Once we got home Cindy and I were sent to our rooms. I tried to apologize through my tears, but it was no use. To me it was only a box of crackers, but to Grandma it was so much more. I don't remember crying a lot as a child; I had no reason to. But on this day I bawled my eyes out until Grandma Lorraine forgave me.

She was quick to overcome her anger and wasn't the type of woman to hold a grudge. She was very forgiving and loving and taught me that a heart full of anger has no room for love.

Aside from the Wheat Thins incident, life was good. I was happy, doing well, and living a carefree existence just being a kid. Grandma, Aunt Betty, Cindy, and I had created our own perfect family.

Somewhere around my sixth birthday, Vicky came back into our lives. She showed up with her new husband, Richard, as if they had merely gone out for milk a few hours before. Vicky and Richard tried to explain to Cindy and me that they were our mom and dad. I was so completely confused because Grandma never corrected us when we called her Mom. She wouldn't have intentionally lied to us, but I think she didn't know when or if Vicky was ever coming back. She knew that all little girls need their moms, and she was more than happy to fill those shoes.

I wondered who these strangers were who wanted to take us away from Grandma, our mommy. I tried to understand what they were saying but I couldn't grasp that not only was Grandma not Mom but that I could no longer live with her.

I started to worry and my thoughts began drifting. I wondered if Grandma Lorraine would have enough money, if she would be OK without us. Cindy and I had always been there for her. Who would take care of Grandma?

I instantly knew life would never be the same, but I had no idea how topsy-turvy it would become. All I knew was that this young, beautiful woman and tall, handsome man had come to take us away from Grandma Lorraine. I was aware enough to know it wasn't normal, but too young to do anything about it.

Grandma had taught me to be a respectful little lady, to never talk back to adults, and to always do as I was told. When Vicky asked me to gather my things and bring them to her car, I did—no questions asked. But it was incomprehensible that

Grandma was hugging and kissing me goodbye. With tears in her eyes, she reminded me to watch over and take care of Cindy. As she hugged me, I told her if she needed money for food, she could take the $89 in my savings account. It may sound odd for a 6-year-old child to worry about such things, but I understood the value of money. I also knew Grandma Lorraine didn't have a lot of it and was careful about the future.

I don't remember my own tears. I know there was no kicking or screaming. There were no tantrums or drama. It was just a quiet parting from a wonderful, stable life full of love and affection.

I sat in the backseat of Richard's car, staring at the empty Coca-Cola bottles and discarded food wrappers on the floor. Grandma's car was always pristine and clean. I was overwhelmed by the unfamiliar emotions I was feeling and by the lump in my throat that I couldn't swallow. I sat paralyzed, unable to even look back to see my grandma's sweet face and whether she was waving goodbye. I couldn't move. I was frozen, still in my grief and silence.

I couldn't bear the pain of my loss. I naturally began the process of not sharing my emotions so no one could tell I was hurting. Even though I was sad and overwhelmed, I wanted to be strong for Cindy because I understood this wasn't the way to start our new life.

Vicky and Richard took us to their small apartment above a garage off Venice Boulevard in Marina del Rey, just a short distance from Grandma Lorraine. Not long after, Vicky's father, Grandpa Paul, co-signed for a house on Yale Street that Richard wanted to buy. It was a pretty green house with a huge tree in the front yard.

On weekends Grandpa Paul used to make a special trip to come pick Cindy and me up. We called it "Grandpa Day." He had a big convertible and always wanted to take us for a ride to his favorite cigar shop. As he picked out his beloved cigars, my sister and I had our own special mission—to pick out our candy treat. For Cindy and me it was always the same, a box of Good & Plenty. It was a soft black licorice candy coated in a hard shell. Black, pink, and white, just like the packaging. I could never decide my favorite color to eat first. Cindy and I would sit in the front seat of Grandpa's car, with the top down and the sun shining bright like it always does in Southern California.

Grandpa Paul drove with his elbow resting on the door, puffing away on his big cigar, grinning from ear to ear as the wind blew back our long blond hair. He always managed to find our favorite song on the radio—the Archies' "Sugar, Sugar."

"Sugar.
Do do do do do do.
Awww. Honey honey.
Do do do do do do.
You are my candy girl!"

He chuckled as we sang at the top of our lungs and shook our candy boxes like tambourines along to the music.

Although Grandpa Paul was a gambler and had a long history of being hard on his wife, Grandma Dicie, he was always gentle and sweet to us. He thoroughly enjoyed spending his time with Cindy and me. It was hard to imagine him being mean and nasty to anyone. To me he was pure fun.

At first life with Vicky and Richard was a great adventure. They were young and hip. Vicky had beautiful red hair, which she wore midway down her back. When she got dressed up, she wore either a fashionable wig, a fabulous hair fall, or a pinned-in updo. She stood about 5 feet 6 inches and dressed in stylish, chic clothes, which showed off her fantastic, slim figure.

Richard was as striking as Vicky, with a full head of dark wavy hair, bright eyes, tall, and slender but muscular. He often wore T-shirts and jeans and sported a wide smile with a mouthful of white teeth.

If you need me, call me. No matter where you are, no matter how far, you can depend on me and never worry.
"Ain't No Mountain High Enough"
Words and music by Nickolas Ashford and Valerie Simpson

Vicky and Richard were much cooler than anyone I had ever met. They loved trendy music, which was anything but Lawrence Welk or the Chipmunks. Diana Ross and the Supremes were all the rage. "Ain't No Mountain High Enough" became our naptime lullaby. To this day, anytime I hear that song, I reach for the phone to call Cindy.

Shortly after we moved into the house on Yale Street, Vicky gave birth to my sister Kimmy. She was a chubby baby with blond curly hair that looked like golden coiled springs attached to her head. She was the most beautiful baby, and I thought she looked just like Shirley Temple. She was the first child Vicky and Richard had together, and it was nice to see them connect through a baby. Kimmy brought us all together as a family. In fact it was the best time we ever shared.

Our first Christmas together was spent baking cookies with Vicky, waiting for Richard to come home from work so we could open our presents. He strutted through the door like

Elvis Presley, giving Vicky a loving peck on the cheek as he snapped up a freshly baked cookie.

That Christmas there was no Grandma Lorraine. Vicky and Richard were adamant that she could no longer be a presence in my sister's and my life. They wanted to get as far away from her influence as possible. I couldn't understand why she wasn't allowed to come over to see us and why we were no longer allowed to see her. I couldn't imagine what Grandma had done wrong. If we weren't being punished, then she certainly was.

Maybe they were jealous of the bond that Cindy and I shared with her. Maybe I shouldn't have told Vicky I called Grandma "Mommy," or perhaps they resented the fact that she always tried to encourage our relationship with Wayne, whom they did not like.

Although he never laid a hand on me, Wayne had a history of being abusive to both Grandma Lorraine and Vicky. From what I was told, his wrath was swift and terrible. They said he could explode on a moment's notice, especially if he had been drinking. I'm sure, in their youth and limited experience, Vicky and Richard believed separating my sister and me from that family was in our best interest. I don't remember them ever talking about their actual reasons, so I never really knew the truth.

Vicky and Richard were only about 23 years old, but they already had three kids. They were trying to make the best decisions they could at that stage in their lives—at least that's what I thought. Now that I look back, I think they simply lacked the wisdom and experience to make better choices. Lessons that came easily to Grandma Lorraine had yet to be learned by them.

Vicky and Richard had a way of glossing over important issues, refusing to discuss certain matters, and ignoring my questions. Everything Grandma had taught me about sharing and communication, the importance of relationships, and working together as a family was quickly unraveling in my new home. So I stopped asking questions altogether.

Chapter Two
Stunned Into Silence

We had joy, we had fun, we had seasons in the sun.

Terry Jacks

I slowly began adjusting to my new life with Vicky and Richard, which was truly pretty fun at first. After all, Los Angeles is a great place to grow up, and every day seems like summer to a 6-year-old. I was a tanned, blond beach baby who spent most afternoons in dune buggies and most nights around bonfires at the edge of the ocean. Vicky and Richard loved to barbecue with other couples who gathered to party every weekend on the crowded shore.

One night I accidentally wandered away from Vicky while she was busy talking with her friends. The sun was going down, and the magic of twilight reflected off the sea, turning the sky a light blue and purple. I was enchanted by the beauty of the beach at night. The warm summer sea foam washed over my bare feet as I walked along the shore in search of seashells. When I looked up I didn't recognize where I was or anyone around me. I desperately tried to navigate the masses of people who dotted the beach, uncertain if I would ever find our party again.

No one looked familiar.

I was frozen with fear. I was absolutely alone and, worse yet, I knew it.

I searched high and low on the sand. I walked up to the winding bike path that paralleled the beach and stopped near the Santa Monica pier. I was familiar with the pier because Richard used to take me for boat rides in the rough surf below.

A policeman found me wandering in a beach parking lot and asked where my parents were. I couldn't tell him. The officer took my hand and walked me from bonfire to bonfire until he reunited me with Vicky. I don't recall her even being aware that I had gone missing.

I sat in front of the bright, warm bonfire next to Cindy, thankful to be with her. Still dewy-eyed I stared into the flames, thinking the beach must be full of angels like the officer who saved me that night.

A week or so before I got lost, I had gone out with Richard on his inflatable raft. When we were done I had to climb a tall ladder to get onto the top of the pier. It felt as if that ladder went high up into the sky and that I would never reach the top, afraid to look down for fear I would fall. I finally reached the top and looked back to see if Richard was coming behind me. The buzzing energy on the pier was overwhelming. There were loud carnival rides, arcade games, and noisy crowds of people everywhere. I was scared because I had just climbed onto a boardwalk of chaos. I began to walk away from all of the noises and unknowingly backed myself up to the pier's edge. I nearly lost my footing when I suddenly felt a strong hand grab me from behind. At first I didn't know who was touching me. Only afterward did I realize this angel on earth had just saved my life by stopping me from falling into the ocean.

I stood speechless as he began yelling at me for being so reckless. I had never heard anyone shout so loudly, and certainly not directly at me. His voice was thunderous, searing the words "BE MORE CAREFUL" into my mind. Since leaving Grandma's house it was by far the most traumatic event in my childhood. Up to this point, there had been no volatility, no chaos, and no loud voices. Everything was calm, peaceful, and lovely.

Until we moved to the state of Washington.

Sometime around 1972 Richard announced he'd been transferred to Washington for his job as a computer programmer. It seemed as if we had just moved into the house on Yale Street in Marina Del Rey and before I knew it, we were on the move for the third time since reuniting as a family.

When I first found out we were moving, I was excited because Vicky and Richard promised we would see snow. Since I had never experienced a real winter, the notion sounded simply wonderful. Watching *Frosty the Snowman* was as close to snow as I had ever been. Besides, my newfound excitement masked the loss I felt with the absence of Grandma Lorraine. I wanted to call and tell her the exciting news, but that wasn't an option.

Vicky and Richard weren't the type of parents to sit down and explain anything to us. They just packed up our stuff, loaded it into the truck, and put Cindy, Kimmy, and me in the backseat. We made the 17-hour drive straight through. I was mesmerized by the beauty of the mountains and the picturesque landscape of Northern California and the Oregon coast. I had never seen anything but sunshine and desert.

We pulled into the small town of Sumner, which looked like the set of *It's a Wonderful Life* with its storybook main street decorated for the holiday season. I could see my breath as I oohed and aahed at the beauty of this small town. There were shiny, glittery silver bells, golden scrolls, and trumpeting white angels strung high above a street that seemed to go on forever. There was snow on the sidewalks that glistened in the evening light. It was a magical fairy tale. I thought it was a slice of heaven.

When we arrived we lived in two small motel rooms that were connected as a suite until Richard could find us a proper home. The motel was dark and cramped. It was an older building with filthy cheap furniture, weird lighting, and bad art on the walls. There was musty shag carpeting on the floors that looked as if it hadn't been cleaned in years. There was a pullout sofa in the living room, where my sisters and I slept under a yucky nylon bedspread to keep warm. It was nothing like Grandma's house.

It was during those first few weeks in the motel that I first noticed Vicky was sleeping more than usual. She hardly ever got out of bed during the day and rarely changed her nightgown.

A few months after we arrived in Sumner, Richard finally found us a house. It was a light blue two-story house with the Puyallup River running through our backyard. There were four bedrooms, two bathrooms, a living room, a dining room, and kitchen. It wasn't large but it sure beat the motel. The yard was huge and the landscaping was lovely. There were a long row of Chinese cherry trees in the backyard along the bank of the river and lots of beauty bark. In fact, Richard built a pathway down to the water out of railroad ties he found at the town hardware and feed store.

Vicky enrolled Cindy and me at the local elementary school down the street. Kimmy was still a baby, so she stayed home during the day. When we came back from school, we usually found Vicky in the exact same position we had left her in. I just thought she was being lazy. I didn't understand why she was so lethargic. When I realized she was pregnant with my brother Richie, a new and much needed excitement was brought into our home. By the time Richie was born in May of 1973, Vicky's mood was becoming unpredictable and gradually more volatile. It must have been overwhelming for her to have four children by the age of 25. Her quickness of temper and shortness of patience became greater by the day.

The only time Vicky yelled at me before we moved to Washington was one morning when I couldn't find my shoes. We had all overslept, and I was late for school. Vicky and Richard were livid that I couldn't remember where I had left them.

Vicky kept saying I was so disorganized and screaming, "Where the hell are they?"

I vividly recall the word "hell" because Grandma Lorraine never swore. Grandma would have hated that word being used in her house. It wasn't Christian. I thought I had done something really terrible for Vicky to be yelling and swearing. Vicky's reaction left a lasting impact. To this day I make it a point to always be organized.

After Richie was born Vicky became increasingly depressed. I grew up describing her illness as being "sick." I didn't understand that she was in fact mentally ill. The more depressed she got, the less work she could do around the house. By the time I was 8 years old, Richard was working most of the time, so when I wasn't at school, I spent my afternoons doing chores.

I helped with the laundry, went to the grocery store, helped cook, cleaned up, and watched the kids.

Cindy and I never spoke about our new life because we didn't have to. We could look at each other across the room or in the backseat of Richard's truck and acknowledge that everything was different. We didn't know what to say, so we didn't say anything. I escaped into silence, overwhelmed with the responsibility of being the oldest of four kids.

I don't remember Vicky working when we were kids. She had been raised precious and pampered by her parents. This was very different from Grandma Lorraine who worked constantly to make ends meet. Richard had a good job, but I thought all moms also worked outside the home. Not Vicky—she had never worked and that didn't change when she married Richard. She always lived a life of ease as her parents' favorite child. Of course this changed slightly when she and Richard became Jehovah's Witnesses after we moved to Washington. I found the religion to be very confusing, a dramatic contrast to the religion Grandma Lorraine lived by. But Vicky and Richard were Jehovah's Witnesses, and that was now our faith.

As Jehovah's Witnesses we were not allowed to interact with people who did not share our beliefs. Holidays were no longer allowed, which meant no Christmas, no birthdays, no Halloween, and no Easter. As a kid this meant no fun. Other than weddings and anniversaries, celebrations of any kind were all but prohibited. There were no pictures, no happy memories, and no heirloom traditions. This cut out the normal joys of childhood that I grew up experiencing with Grandma.

There was usually an outing after services every Sunday, which we always attended. I became friends with the other children my age in the congregation. They were the only kids I was allowed to play with. As Vicky became friendlier with the other Witness women, she frequently offered her personal items to the children of those women as a gesture of friendship and generosity. I wanted Vicky to pass her things on to me. I was her daughter, her oldest child. Although I felt unappreciated and hurt, I never said a word. And she never gave me a thing—not even her old set of hair rollers, which I wanted most of all.

Mothers are supposed to pass their possessions on to their daughters as Grandma had done with us. But that was not Vicky. She'd sooner give another child her things before her children. Vicky seemed to invest her generosity—both her emotional adoration and her personal possessions—in others, not her family and clearly not me.

Vicky's mother, Dicie, was a very beautiful, glamorous seamstress to the stars. She was tall and had fabulous cheekbones, great eyes, and jet-black hair. She looked like the movie stars she dressed in her couture. Esther Williams was one of her most important clients. Vicky's sister, Aunt Peggy, was Grandma Dicie's fit model. She was a perfect size 2. She always had the most beautiful clothes in school. Grandma Dicie's husband, Grandpa Paul, was a gambler and squandered his money. He became so reckless that he eventually lost Grandma Dicie's business and their marriage along with it.

When Vicky left Cindy and me with Grandma Lorraine, Aunt Peggy and her husband, Uncle Bill, tried to adopt us because they weren't able to have children of their own. Vicky always seemed terribly jealous of Peggy and would never have shared her children. Aunt Peggy and Uncle Bill loved us as if we were their own and wanted to provide us a good life. They would often come pick up Cindy and me for weekend sleepovers when Grandma had to work and Aunt Betty was unavailable.

Though Aunt Peggy and Uncle Bill weren't wealthy, they were stable, kind, and generous to my sister and me. They were always available and often invited us to visit them back in California, and even paid for our travel to see them. When she was around, Aunt Peggy often took me on trips to the mall.

When I was 12, I had my eye on a trendy cotton dress with crisscrossing straps in the back and buttons down to the waistline. It was the most popular and fashionable dress of that year, and I wanted it more than anything. Vicky had already said she wouldn't buy it for me, so I knew it would never be mine.

As we walked past the racks of clothing, Aunt Peggy could tell I really wanted the dress. Though I never said a word, she must have sensed my intense desire to have it. She suddenly turned to me and asked, "Do you want that dress?"

I was stunned.

"Well, go ahead and pick one out," she said. "I'd love to buy one for you, sweetie."

No one had ever bought me anything so beautiful or so expensive. The dress cost almost $50. Her kindness meant the world to me. The dress was mine, and no one could take it away. She made it clear to me how important my happiness was to her.

I felt beautiful when I wore the dress later that day. I feathered my hair like Farrah Fawcett, blew it dry, hair sprayed it into place, and did everything I could to look like the quintessential

California girl. But, in the end, it wasn't about the dress, the hair, or the money. It was about being back in California with family who unconditionally loved me and spending an enjoyable afternoon with my aunt and not having a care in the world.

When we first moved to Washington, Richard tried to be a family guy. He spent a lot of time maintaining the house and working on the landscaping to make it beautiful. He seemed to care about us and, for a while, even showed me his kind side. Sadly, it didn't last long.

When I got very lonely and scared, I would sneak downstairs late at night to call Grandma Lorraine. I missed her so much. When I phoned she always told me to hang up and call her back collect. I didn't want my phone calls to cost her money, so I never did. Vicky and Richard discovered my secret midnight calls when their phone bill arrived. They were furious that I defied their wishes and I had to be punished.

I had never been physically hit before we moved to Washington. Looking back, Richard would jokingly say he would like to have a house where he could beat his children without the neighbors hearing.

By the time I was 9, Richard had introduced me to his belt. He would rip that black leather strap off his pants, fold it in half, and snap it a few times to let me know what was coming. The sight of the belt in his hands made me feel sick with terror. I never understood what I had done wrong. Richard believed that his philosophy of "Spare the rod and spoil the child" was supported by our new religious practices: This is how you train children and make them understand the consequences of every bad action. I didn't want to be spoiled, so I figured I must have deserved it.

The belt left marks across the backs of my legs. I wore tights to hide the bruises, but they were obvious for anyone to see. When I told a friend at school about the beatings, she couldn't understand what I was saying. Her parents did not believe in hitting their children.

A few days later a school nurse called me into her office for a mandatory school physical. She told me to go behind the curtain, take off all my clothes, and come back out for an examination. As I disrobed I realized she would see the black and blue marks across the back of my legs and bottom. I didn't want to risk getting in trouble again. I was terrified the nurse would discover the marks, phone my parents, and ask questions. I refused to show her my backside, going out of my way to only face forward as she did her best to examine me. I'm certain the nurse knew something was wrong, but she couldn't prove a thing because I never let her see. In those days school systems didn't get as involved in a child's home life as they do today.

Richard's behavior opened the door for Vicky to vent her anger on us as well. She used a wooden spoon. It was easier for her to handle and surprisingly stung more. She once hit Cindy so hard that the spoon actually broke, leaving a large wooden shard embedded in my sister's thigh. Vicky refused to take Cindy to the doctor, surely knowing what she had done was wrong and afraid they might discover what had happened. A week later Cindy couldn't sit because her thigh was so infected. Vicky was forced to take her to the doctor.

On the way Vicky coached Cindy on what to say if the doctor started asking questions. "Tell him you fell and a sliver of wood got stuck in your skin."

Cindy did as she was told.

I felt sorry for Cindy because it was obvious she was terrified. When Vicky made Cindy lie, it was the first time I realized she knew her abusive actions were wrong. My brother, sisters, and I lived in a constant state of fear, walking on eggshells, uncertain about what would set her off. Every time Vicky walked past me, I would wince and flinch, worried she might hit me. I often put my hands up to protect my face just in case she decided to let loose. Whenever I did she would give me a malicious smirk to remind me that she was the one in control and that I was there to serve her.

Chapter Three
A Child in Charge

How children survive being brought up amazes me.
Malcolm S. Forbes

Life had become a daily struggle to avoid Vicky's and Richard's volatile outbursts. I was 9 years old, and as Vicky's mental illness slowly incapacitated her, I became the sole caretaker of our family.

I didn't sleep much as a kid. Maybe it was because of the mounting pressures and growing tensions between Vicky and Richard.

One night I heard crying coming from Vicky's bedroom. She was in her second trimester of another pregnancy and had become extremely emotional. Although Richard was away on a business trip, Vicky was convinced he was off cheating on her. She often drew me into their relationship problems as if I were her best friend. She'd ask my advice as if I were an experienced adult, but I was only a confused kid who didn't understand what was going on.

At the time I actually believed Richard was the source of all of Vicky's problems. I thought he was the reason she was constantly miserable. I couldn't understand why she was taking so much Valium and Vicodin. I was completely protective of Vicky and I never considered the idea that she was responsible for her own actions and her own destiny. It never entered my mind that she could be the main cause of her illness.

Vicky's crying intensified when she saw me walk into the bathroom. To my horror she was on the bathroom floor doubled over, with blood everywhere. She was having a miscarriage. I instantly felt sick to my stomach.

Although I was only 9, I knew how to call for an ambulance. Luckily the paramedics got there quickly. She seemed to be very weak from the blood loss and emotionally distraught from the trauma.

After the ambulance came I did my best to clean up the mess. I washed the sheets, changed the bed, and wiped the floor the best I could. I was traumatized when the thought finally occurred to me that she could have died. When Vicky came home a couple of days later, she acted as if nothing had happened. I don't remember ever speaking of the incident again.

By the time I was 10, Vicky and Richard were fighting all the time. I absorbed all of their tension whenever I sat in the backseat of our old green station wagon on the way home from services or in a room with them while they argued. The tension was so thick it could be cut with a knife. Whenever I was in the car with them, it took everything I had to keep calm. I didn't know what I was feeling at the time, but I began having anxiety attacks. These attacks stunned me into a quiet stillness.

I began biting and chewing my nails until they bled. As a result I became horribly self-conscious of my fingers. I always folded them under the palms of my hands or hid them in my pockets. I never wanted anyone to see what the uncontrollable habit was doing to me. I couldn't stop because I had no other outlet for my stress.

In spite of everything, Vicky became pregnant again and my brother Johnny was born around my 11th birthday. Richard felt incredibly guilty for not being home when Vicky lost the previous baby, so he was much more attentive during this pregnancy. I believe he truly wanted to salvage their relationship. Things turned around for a while, but it wasn't long before Vicky became depressed and started taking her pills again.

Richard had finally had enough and knew it was time to leave. He couldn't take living with Vicky any longer. He soon began a relationship with a woman named Terry. Around this time my parents were excommunicated from our congregation, and Richard decided to move to Oregon to start a new life with Terry and her two children.

Vicky spiraled downward after Richard left. Overnight things went from bad to worse. When Vicky was younger, she suffered an injury that broke her nose. I don't recall how it happened, but I do remember she used a lot of 4-Way nasal spray so she could breathe. Eventually the 4-Way wasn't strong enough, so she changed to Neo-Synephrine, which seemed to work better. The only reason I can remember the names of these products is because she used to scream for them at the top of her lungs as she stumbled back and forth from her bedroom to the living room couch.

I was overwhelmed by the responsibilities that fell to me. By age 12 I was doing all the laundry, cooking, cleaning, and grocery shopping. I was the only one available to help the kids with their homework and put them to bed at night. There were six of us in the house, but I was the one handling most of the load. I would come home from school and find huge piles of laundry that had to be done. I seemed to be swimming in piles of dirty clothes, sink loads full of dishes, and every room in the house that looked as if it had been hit by a hurricane. By the time I got as much done as I could, I didn't have time to do my schoolwork, let alone anything else. I desperately wanted to be in the school Christmas concert or even get to have sleepovers with friends. Instead, I was busy looking after my brothers and sisters as if they were my own children. Cindy was the only one who was old enough to help out and she did as much as she could.

A good day was making sure Cindy, Kimmy, Richie, and Johnny were safe and sound. I'd like to tell you I was perfect at it, but I wasn't. Lots of times it was just too much for me.

There were many scary moments when life felt completely out of control. Such as the time when Johnny was 3 and wandered off our property, up the road, and onto a heavily traveled two-lane highway. One of our neighbors found him on the side of the road holding onto a rake that he'd placed across the road. When the neighbor asked what he was doing, Johnny explained, "I want to trip a car with my rake."

I could barely breathe when I found out what happened. I can still remember the unbelievable look of disgust on my neighbor's face. For weeks following this near disaster, every time I closed my eyes I saw my brother standing on the side of the road holding his rake. I had visions of him being hit by a car and flying into the field.

Then there was the time that Richie lifted the heat vent from the floor, leaving a hole that he accidentally fell into.

The metal side of the vent was so sharp that it slit open his calf, leaving a gash that required several stitches.

I daydreamed of being a normal kid, but that wasn't the reality in which I lived. My life had become hell. I knew my grandma would be ashamed if she even knew I was thinking that word. I never spoke it out loud, but that's how I felt.

I lie here buried alive in my loneliness.

Friedrich Nietzsche

Everything had changed for us when we moved to Washington. We no longer had the support of our extended family. We socialized with no one—not even our neighbors or our congregation.

After Vicky and Richard separated, we didn't have enough money to live, certainly not the way we did with Richard. Although he paid child support, it wasn't enough money for all of us to survive. Grandma Lorraine had started sending Vicky money to help supplement our expenses. I felt so bad for Grandma, having taken us in and then being completely cut off, only to feel the need to support us even though she hadn't been allowed to see us in years. I can only imagine how excited she must have felt knowing that if she gave Vicky money, she would be able to see Cindy and me again.

Vicky spent most of her days on the couch watching soap operas. All she seemed to do was use her nasal spray, take her pills, and scream at me. As a result we were forced to go on welfare and collect food stamps so we could eat.

Vicky and I went down to the welfare office to fill out the paperwork. We sat in uncomfortable plastic chairs that lined the long, sterile corridor, waiting for someone to explain the system to us. I looked around thinking we didn't belong there. The other people had a look of desperation in their eyes I never wanted to see coming from another human being. They seemed lost and alone. I didn't want to think of myself that way. I never felt lost, though there were many times I felt alone. It was hard to look at the other recipients and believe I was like them. However, there I was, waiting just like them. I never said a word to Vicky. I just helped her fill out form after endless form so we could get the money and food stamps.

A woman finally met with us to go over the rules of using food stamps. She said we could not buy cigarettes or paper goods such as toilet paper, paper towels, plastic trash bags, or diapers. Those items had to be paid for with the cash out of our welfare check. We could buy cheese, milk, meat, and anything that was a consumable food product. I still remember her exact terminology. Being on welfare is something I will never forget.

After we left the welfare office, Vicky took me to McDonald's. I thought that would be the last time I would be having a Big Mac, my favorite fast food.

Along with the food stamps, Vicky was issued a prescription medical card that allowed her to get drugs and services from various doctors at a very low cost. The doctors always gave her whatever she asked for, not knowing that there were multiple physicians writing the same prescriptions.

I had become mom, sister, caretaker, and homemaker of our family. Managing our new lifestyle under such a tight budget was a tremendous responsibility. When the welfare check arrived at the beginning of every month, Vicky would sign the back and I'd take my bicycle up to the bank to make the deposit. I'd ride through the drive-through lane and stuff the deposit into the plastic cylinder that popped out of the metal box.

I'd take the food stamps to the local store and stock the kitchen the best I could. Sometimes Vicky gave me a shopping list, but mostly it was up to me to stretch the limited buying capacity I had shopping with food stamps. I rode my bike to the store with the food stamps to buy the things we needed. On the way home I had to ride very carefully so that the full plastic bags hanging from my handlebars wouldn't swing and break the eggs. If we had extra expenses, or even if we were $5 short, that meant we wouldn't be eating for the last few days of the month. I had to ration our food to ensure we had something every day. I was so glad Grandma had taught me to be frugal and how to cook because there was no other way for us to make it through. We made simple bargain cuisine, not because we wanted to, but because we had to.

At the beginning of every month, we ate a lot of fried chicken, tacos, and burgers. By the end of the month, it was anything I could create out of cornmeal. I made cornmeal loaves, which I sliced, fried, and served to the kids like pancakes with maple syrup. They were surprisingly delicious, but, more important, they were very filling. I also became the queen of corn dogs, which the kids loved!

One day Social Services knocked on our door. At the time, I didn't even know what a social worker was. Vicky was told an anonymous caller reported abuse and neglect. I was sure it was our neighbors, Pat and Carl. Their son Mark was my dearest friend and knew what my everyday life had become.

Mark knew I was being hit and saw that I was trying to run the entire household. Even though he witnessed how hard and different life was in our home, it didn't scare him. Mark was always there to offer his help.

Vicky pulled herself together long enough to satisfy the visiting social worker by convincing her she only had the flu. Her performance must have been Oscar-worthy because the social worker never came back. I don't know what happened, but she was obviously convinced that we were all fine and living in a happy and healthy home.

I was thrilled with the outcome because I feared that foster care would be far worse than our current conditions. Vicky reminded me every chance she got that she would send me away to live with foster parents or, worse, a juvenile detention center if I didn't obey her. I wasn't to talk to my teachers or any other adults about my life at home. It was a threat that haunted me and the thought was terrible and terrorizing.

Doing what Vicky asked never seemed to be enough. She often sent me to the store to buy something she wanted or needed. I never thought much of it. I was happy to have a few minutes of peace and solitude away from the chaotic environment at home. One particular afternoon Vicky was craving a Chunky candy bar, so she told me to ride my bike to the local convenience store and buy her one. I thought it would be nice to surprise the other kids with a treat too. When I got to the store, I was mortified to discover they were out of Chunky bars. I bought several alternatives I thought Vicky might like, but I knew she wouldn't take the news well.

I had the worst feeling in my stomach as I slowly pedaled my bike back to the house without her candy.

Then I had a great idea.

I would buy her a small bouquet of flowers instead. Surely she would understand it wasn't my fault that the store didn't have her candy. What mom wouldn't be delighted with a bouquet of pretty flowers from her child? It was a perfect plan. At least that's what I thought until I walked through the door.

I ran to my bedroom to fill out the card for Vicky before I gave her the flowers. I placed the bouquet on the floor right behind my door. Before I could finish her card, Vicky pushed the door open and walked in.

"Where's my candy?" she asked.

I trembled and fumbled my words, trying to explain the store was out of Chunky bars. I handed over the bag of candy I bought.

"What's all this?" she asked. "I told you to get me a Chunky bar."

Again I attempted to tell her the store didn't have any, but she didn't want to hear it.

"Yes they did. I called myself, and they said they had Chunky bars!" she yelled. Before I could respond, Vicky stepped forward and backhanded me across the face. On her way out of the room, she noticed the flowers on the floor.

"What is that?" she asked.

I tried to speak through my tears. "I bought them for you because I couldn't get you the Chunky bar."

Vicky just glared at me and then stormed out of my room.

I finally realized I would never make her happy. It didn't matter how much laundry I did, or how many times I cooked dinner or did the dishes. It would never be enough to satisfy her.

To be fair it wasn't just me who made Vicky mad. She felt trapped and betrayed. She was angry that she didn't live in California anymore. She had only agreed to move to Washington for Richard, and now that he was gone, she resented being there. She felt unattractive, alone, and completely depressed.

Vicky wasn't some evil stepmother who came into our lives—she was our mom. But for me my real mom lived on Grant Street in Santa Monica, where everything was neat, clean, and organized. At Grandma Lorraine's house there was only consistent kindness and love.

I began to feel sad for Vicky. She had five beautiful children who were all wonderful, well behaved, smart, loving, and caring. She never had the benefit of knowing how special her life could have been by just being our mom.

The welfare check simply wasn't enough to make ends meet, so I had to figure out how to make some extra money. Unfortunately, at 13, I wasn't old enough to get a work permit, so I had to find other ways. I had Cindy take care of the kids while I cleaned other people's houses. I made $10 here and $15 there doing laundry, raking leaves, and taking out garbage. I never said no to any job.

I was always good at arts and crafts and found it relaxing. It reminded me of my time at Grandma's house. I was passionate about the items I made and was careful to make sure they were pretty and perfect. I could create cute knickknacks quickly and with very little money. I started making hand-loomed pot holders out of nylon loops and sold those door-to-door around the neighborhood for a dollar a pair. During the Christmas season I made fragrant holiday angel wallhangings from fabric remnants, cotton balls, and sticks, which I tied together with yarn.

My love for arts and crafts comes from my earliest childhood memories of making sweet, sentimental things for Grandma that made her house feel homey.

My best friend Mark and I used to go down to the river behind my house and find old pieces of driftwood that we'd glue plastic squirrels, deer, moss, and faux trees onto, which emulated a forestscape. The finished product was woodsy and cute. We sold our outdoor art for $25! That was a lot of money for us kids. Not only did we cover our costs, but we also had plenty of profit left over to share.

Mark and I also went to the local golf course to collect lost balls, which we sold back to the golfers for a couple of bucks a bucket. It was an annuity business to us budding entrepreneurs because we could recycle those same old balls several times a day. Bad golfers were our friends!

I picked bunches of wild daffodils in the vacant field across the highway from our house and sold them on the side of the road. When berry season started, Mark and I had a lot of fun gathering strawberries, raspberries, blueberries, and cherries in the fields. We even got into berry fights from time to time, pelting each other with mushy red strawberries. It was a festive food fight. Every week throughout the summer, I brought home at least $40 a day from selling berries.

You might think this was the beginning of the future entrepreneur in me, but it really wasn't. It was about making money to survive. On Friday I would hand over what I had made to Vicky. I was proud of my accomplishment and happy to help.

I thought life was getting better. I was making money and Cindy was able to help by taking care of the kids. I no longer had time to notice that Vicky was more depressed than ever.

Late one night Vicky walked into the kitchen with tears rolling down her face. She must have been crying for a long time as her eyes were completely swollen. I had just finished doing the dishes when I saw Vicky grab one of the freshly cleaned glasses from the counter and fill it with water. She began to swallow an entire bottle of pills. I was frantically begging her to stop.

I also began crying uncontrollably. It was obvious that she was trying to kill herself.

I quickly dialed 911. I wondered how long it took for a bottle of pills to kick in and whether she would die. Once again the paramedics were at our house in an instant.

They immediately took Vicky to the ambulance. I heard one of the paramedics say they had to pump her stomach. I couldn't get the image out of my mind. All I could conjure up was a toilet plunger being put inside her.

The ambulance soon pulled out of our driveway and raced down the road with its siren blaring and lights flashing. I stood in front of the house and stared off into the distance until the siren faded to silence. I didn't know how to explain what happened to the kids, so I just told them Vicky was sick.

We remained in the house alone for three days. During that time I don't recall anyone coming to check on us.

I sat, staring out the window, watching the storms that blow through Washington come and go. I had no one to talk to, so I got lost in my thoughts of our future. I was trying to reconcile everything leading up to that day. I didn't understand Vicky's darkness or how to help her. To be honest, I was so tired that a part of me imagined what it would be like if she didn't come home.

One afternoon I heard what sounded like a large truck barreling down our road. And then I heard brakes screeching and a loud thump! One of the neighbor's horses had broken loose and had run into the road. The trucker never saw the horse before he accidentally sent the animal flying 50 feet into the cornfield in front of our home.

When I realized this beautiful, powerful horse had been killed, I couldn't contain my emotion. Perhaps there was safety in knowing Vicky was miles away and wouldn't see me in my own moment of weakness. Maybe it was a way to purge my feelings about watching her try to end her life. Whatever the reason, I cried and cried until I had no more tears. And then it was over. I had come to terms with the fact that Grandma was gone, Richard was gone, and I was alone.

My dreams were all my own; I accounted for them to nobody; they were my refuge when annoyed—my dearest pleasure when free.   *Mary Wollstonecraft Shelley*

When Vicky returned home she was placed in an outpatient treatment program so she could get the help she needed. She sat me down and explained that she had had what the doctors referred to as a nervous breakdown. She apologized for taking the pills and then admitted she was very sick. I always understood that Vicky suffered from an illness. I just couldn't identify it as depression. Now I knew about her affliction, but I couldn't focus on her because I had four kids I was looking after who needed my attention more than she did.

We all went back to school that September. At age 13, I had to find a babysitter for Johnny because I didn't think it would be safe to leave him home with Vicky. Every morning before I went off to school, I walked Johnny to a neighboring house that ran an affordable day care. I had no other choice unless I stopped going to school. Johnny cried every single morning. He was too sad for a 3-year-old and there was nothing I could do to fix it.

After the breakdown and without Richard, to some degree life was a little easier for all of us. It was easier but not necessarily better. There was a sense of relief when Richard left because Vicky stopped yelling all the time. Eventually, her old irrational ways returned, and this time with a vengeance.

By now Richard and Terry had broken up, and Richard had moved back to Washington. He came on weekends to visit his kids. Sometimes we even got to spend the weekend at his house. One Friday he had come by for a visit and could see that I was particularly stressed out. I stood in the kitchen and completely lost it. I began to cry as I told Richard about how difficult life had become since he left. Not knowing what to say or how to console me, Richard must have known in that moment that all hell had broken loose. He decided to get me out of the situation and calm me down so that he could understand the full breadth of what I was telling him. He told Vicky he was taking just me that weekend and that we would see her on Sunday.

Richard took me to dinner and then back to his house. By the time we got home, I had shared everything with him and was completely exhausted. Richard put me to bed so I could get a good night's sleep. When I woke up the next morning, he was sleeping next to me but woke as I stirred. He held me like a little girl, stroking my hair and saying he understood how hard things were for me. He spoke with compassion and understanding for the way I had taken care of my family. But

50

somewhere in the conversation his kind and fatherly ways turned a corner and became something very wrong.

I couldn't believe what was happening. I never expected Richard to act in such an inappropriate way. Although he never completed his assault, the experience terrified and disgusted me. It made me feel ashamed. Looking back I think my persistent struggling and yelling must have snapped him into realizing that what he was attempting to do was something I was not interested in. He suddenly stopped and I couldn't get away from him fast enough.

From then on everything was awkward and uncomfortable. Richard tried to make me breakfast, but food was the last thing on my mind. I had no appetite. I just wanted to be away from him and to escape from my life. In an effort to make up for what happened, Richard called Vicky that same morning to tell her she was being too hard on me. He explained she needed to lighten up because I was breaking from the pressure. He really got down on her for not being a good role model or proper mother. The irony was that Vicky expected Richard to talk me into helping out more around the house. It was absurd for anyone to think that a child could have done more than I was already doing.

When I got home I confided in my girlfriend Christy what had happened. She eventually told her mother about the attack. When Christy's mother told Vicky what had happened, she completely denied it, going so far as to say that I made up the whole story.

Vicky could try to deny what happened. Although she had hurt me numerous times in my life, her refusal to acknowledge Richard's bad behavior was devastating to me.

After receiving Christy's mom's call, Vicky walked into my bedroom and looked at me with disdain. She spat out that the only reason Richard had stuck up for me that morning was because of what he had done. Vicky said, "He only felt guilty about his own actions and never believed that you are doing enough to help."

In one breath, she turned around and denied what happened to my friend's mother but admitted his actions when she used it against me. Parents are supposed to protect their children. My own mother failed to protect me when she heard what happened. That was the ultimate betrayal.

It was hard for me to talk to Vicky at all after that incident. The distance between us had become too wide to ever close the gap. We were like strangers living under the same roof. I spent the next two years tiptoeing through the minefield of my home, hoping I wouldn't accidentally trigger one of Vicky's emotional bombs but also looking for a way out.

Chapter Four
More Than Me

Quietness is indeed a sign of strength. But quietness may also help one achieve strength.   *Franz Kafka*

The worst attack from Vicky was the last time she ever hit me. It came on the heels of the only compliment I can ever remember her giving me. I was now 15, and any normal relationship between Richard and me was long gone. By now Vicky and I were barely speaking.

One morning before school Vicky looked me in the eyes and said, "You are going to be so much more than I am when you grow up."

I knew she was absolutely right. There was so much I wanted to say to her that morning, but I held back. I spent most of my childhood refusing to confront her. I kept quiet even when I wanted to scream and yell. This moment didn't seem like an appropriate time to let Vicky know how I truly felt. Anything I said was going to provoke her into a rage. Besides I didn't want to make this situation escalate, so as usual, for the moment I said nothing.

Vicky always said she could tell what I was thinking just by looking at my face. This time I couldn't hide my emotion. She was right. I was going to be so much more than she was in ways she couldn't possibly imagine. I wanted to be the opposite of Vicky. I was going to be kind and nice, generous, supportive and nurturing, thoughtful and disciplined, all the things Grandma Lorraine taught me to be—a lady.

I had reached my final point of frustration and wanted her to know that I was tired of being silent. I stared at her in disgust until I could no longer contain myself and said, "You're right. I *am* going to be more than you."

The tone in my voice was filled with sarcasm and disappointment, conviction and a sense of purpose. The words and the implication came out and stunned us both.

In all of the years I spent on the receiving end of Vicky's and Richard's aggression, I never once fought back. Grandma Lorraine raised me to believe a child should never disrespect her parents. God would think that was horrible, and I never wanted to shame myself in God's eyes. So I never lashed out, even when Vicky hit my siblings or me. I stood by and took my punishment and I watched my brothers and sisters unjustly take theirs without uttering a single word to stop her. But this particular day was different. This was the last time Vicky came after me.

She flew into an uncontrollable rage and grabbed me. When I fell back onto the bottom of the bunkbed that was in my brothers' room, Vicky jumped on top of me. Her punches were landing fast and hard—I could barely catch my breath. I lay there thinking this had to end or I would die. She beat me until she was done.

I was black and blue, and she had given me a bloody nose. Both of my eyes were swollen and my body was covered in welts. There was no way I could go to school looking like I did. I wanted to hide my face from the world, ashamed that it now showed the cuts and bruises that reflected my miserable life.

I had a boyfriend at the time named Duane, and I called and asked him to come get me. When he arrived at the house, he took one look at me and said, "Go pack your stuff."

I moved in with Duane's family until I could figure out what I would do next. They were very kind and welcomed me into their home as if I were one of their own. His mother knew I came from a troubled family and went out of her way to make me feel accepted.

I wanted to sew a new jacket to wear with a borrowed dress to Duane's senior prom. The dress was a formal floor-length sheath dress with oversized puffy sleeves, large pink and burgundy floral print fabric, and a ruffled layered bottom. I was trying so hard to put together an outfit that didn't look used or outdated.

Duane bought me the most beautiful pink rose velvet fabric so I could make a bolero jacket. I tried to sew the jacket from a pattern, but it was very hard to follow all of the directions. The stitching wasn't coming together and it was unwearable.

That was the day I discovered that I had no talent for sewing. Clearly I hadn't inherited Grandma Dicie's skills as a seamstress. I became so frustrated that I abandoned the jacket, leaving it on the dining room table.

I was stunned when I walked back into his house the next day and found it finished. Duane's mother had helped me sew the jacket when I couldn't get it right. She had completed it for me. It was absolutely beautiful. I didn't know how to express my gratitude. No one outside my family had ever shown me that type of kindness. I'm not even sure I ever really said thank you. I was embarrassed and moved beyond words.

Despite my insecurities, I finally felt welcomed and accepted by his family when Duane's mom finished that jacket. I'm not sure his parents truly understood the circumstances of my life but Duane surely did. He was my best friend and I told him everything. He was supportive in every way. He adored my siblings and we often took them with us when we went for rides in his red 1965 Mustang fastback. All I wanted to do was marry him, but he was headed for basic training in the Air Force. I knew I couldn't go with him. I had to leave Washington but was unsure of where to go. I don't know what I would have done without Duane and his family during the rough last days in Washington.

There is a time for departure even when there's no certain place to go.   *Tennessee Williams*

It was my decision to leave Vicky's house. Before Vicky and I had had our last encounter, she had given birth to another son. Having another baby in the house was just too much for me. I thought about contacting Aunt Peggy but finally decided to call Grandma Lorraine for help. Grandma bought Duane and me two plane tickets to Los Angeles to talk about my options. That's when I reconnected with my birth father, Wayne. Grandma told me that Wayne and his girlfriend Patty were moving to Wisconsin and would love to have me come live with them. I told Grandma that I wanted to live with her, but she didn't want me raised in Southern California at my age. She felt it was not a good environment for a teenage girl. We all knew that I needed a fresh start somewhere. I wanted the chance to be a regular teenager without the responsibility of taking care of my brothers and sisters, worrying about putting enough food on the table, stretching our very last dollar, and everything else that had been placed on my shoulders the day Vicky emotionally disappeared.

Grandma had been raised in Wisconsin, a place she described as "God's Country." After a lot of thought and consideration, I decided that was the best place for me to go.

Before I left, Duane and I wanted to spend as much time together as possible. A week before I moved, he took me on a road trip through the Pacific Northwest. We camped all around the peninsulas, explored the Oregon and Washington coastlines, and walked through the forests. We had the most magical time.

Duane said he would send for me when he got settled into the military. We talked about someday owning my dream house. I wanted an A-frame with a smaller attached A-frame on the side for a son and daughter. I envisioned driving a Jeep truck up a long driveway lined with tall pine trees. We'd all live high on a hill overlooking the Oregon coastline. I visualized every detail of our future life together on that trip.

With Duane I could wear my heart on my sleeve but was careful not to let anyone else see just how sad and stressed I had become. Duane could always tell when I was miserable. He knew that certain look I had when I was overwhelmed and things were tough. I would stare at the ground with my chin down. Then Duane would always tilt my chin up with his forefinger and say, "Keep your head up, Sandy. Hold your head high." Whenever he lifted my chin, he lifted my spirits.

I left for Wisconsin the day after we got back from our road trip. I was so sad to be leaving. It was incomprehensible to me to not have to take care of my brothers and sisters and see Duane every day. I couldn't begin to imagine what my life in Wisconsin would be like.

Duane drove me to the Sea-Tac airport. Those were the days when someone could still walk you to the gate, so he accompanied me inside. I had the same lump in my throat that I did the day I had to leave Grandma's house when I was 6 years old. My heart was jumping inside my chest like a trapped bird. I was frantic at the thought of leaving. I cried and cried. Duane reassured me that we would see each other again very soon, but I felt as if I only had a moment to fill a lifetime of memories, and that my life was somehow ending and not beginning. I boarded my red-eye flight. Sometime after the wheels lifted off the runway and the lights in the cabin went down, I sat there in the darkness and knew I was alone.

When I left I set myself free. Richard must have realized how bad the situation had become for me to finally leave. He took Kimmy, Richie, and Johnny to live with him and his new wife. Cindy, who was almost 15, didn't want to come with me, so she went to live with one of her best friends. Vicky's new baby stayed with Vicky. No one ever went back. That is when all of our lives truly began. But the trouble wasn't over.

Chapter Five
Moving to Wisconsin

Well, I've been afraid of changing 'cause I've built my life
around you . . .   *Stevie Nicks, "Landslide"*

I left for Wisconsin on June 30, 1982, three days before
my 16th birthday. The Midwest air was thick and sticky. I didn't
expect Wisconsin to be so hot and humid. It was nearly stifling
when I walked off the plane. I was kindly greeted by Wayne and
Patty, who took me to their townhouse in Onalaska. Wayne and
Patty had no other kids, so I was happy to meet a girl my age
who lived next door with her mom, older sister, and younger
brother. Her name was Cindy, just like my sister. She was very
nice, and we became fast friends. I didn't socialize much back in
Sumner, so it was great to have someone to talk to.

Although Wayne and Patty bickered and quarreled a lot, they
seemed to have a good relationship. I thought they acted more
like siblings than boyfriend and girlfriend. After I got settled
in, for the first time in my life I actually had free time on my
hands. Ironically I didn't know what to do with it. I didn't have
to work, didn't have kids to take care of, and wasn't responsible

for keeping the house in order. It was calming but almost too quiet. I hadn't experienced that type of peace or freedom for 10 years, since the time I lived with Grandma Lorraine.

Getting to know Wayne was awkward. On some days he was energetic and fun, and on others he was erratic and unpredictable. In the beginning I thought he had a great sense of humor because he could easily make me laugh. Other times I thought Wayne could be incredibly selfish. He smoked without any regard for the people around him. I was taken aback by the cases of beer he would buy when we went to the grocery store. He seemed to drink it as fast as he could buy it. One minute the beer was neatly stacked in the fridge, and the next, the cans were in a sloppy pile in the trash.

I don't recall Wayne ever having steady work. He was supposed to find a job painting houses as he did in LA working for Grandpa Al, but he never followed through. At the time I didn't know Grandma Lorraine was sending him money every month to help support us.

Shortly before I arrived in Wisconsin, Grandma Lorraine sold her house on Grant Street for a tidy profit. She bought a smaller, less expensive home and was able to put a couple of hundred thousand dollars in the bank to sustain her modest lifestyle. Grandma was smart about her money and never spent a dime on herself. Coupons and secondhand were a way of life. Wayne wasn't the same way.

Patty was in college when I came to live with them. She and I quickly developed a lovely relationship. She was more of a friend than a parent. Even though Patty was an adult, I found I could talk to her about anything. I felt comfortable and confident with her.

I tried to fit in at my new school, but it was no easy task. I got all dressed up for the first day of my junior year. I looked fashionable in my new white peasant top and matching gypsy skirt that closely resembled a ruffled petticoat. I looked as if I had raided Stevie Nicks' closet. I thought my outfit was really pretty, but the girls in school made fun of me. My West Coast style wasn't playing to their Midwestern clique. The kids at my old school had some knowledge about how hard my life was, so they were always compassionate and nice. I expected the kids at my new school to be just as nice. I was surprised at how mean they were to a new kid just trying to fit in on her first day.

Even though life was getting off to an OK start in Onalaska, the initial excitement of being someplace new had worn off. My freedom now felt like a sentence. I missed my brothers and sisters and Duane very much and I was becoming extremely depressed. Those first few months after going back to school were the only time I ever considered taking my own life. I felt empty, lonely, and sad, and wished I were back with the kids and Duane. I missed them so much. My thoughts scared me. How could I be thinking like Vicky? I wanted to kill myself? Life meant nothing to me?

I began talking to my school counselor at Onalaska High. I instantly bonded with her. She was naturally maternal and I felt safe and understood in her office. She was beautiful and soft-spoken, thoughtful and smart, insightful and patient—everything I could want in a counselor, mentor, advisor, and role model. I wasn't feeling very good about myself. I wasn't wearing makeup, doing my hair, or taking the time to care about how I looked. My counselor suggested I get up a half hour early and doll myself up. She assured me that I would feel much better if I thought I looked pretty.

My counselor helped me realize that my depression was brought on by my discomfort with having so much free time. I had become so conditioned to working hard and accustomed to making my own money that now I was bored, anxious, and becoming overwhelmed by my depression. She suggested I get a part-time job after school.

I had always wanted to work in food service, so I got a job at a Hardee's restaurant to fill my days and do something productive. I suppose watching Grandma Lorraine work in the cafeteria as a kid inspired me. Hardee's had the best BLTs ever. I love anything with bacon, so I was thrilled to be working in a place where I could eat BLTs and burgers every day. It was like heaven after living on food stamps for so long.

One of my most vivid memories about living in Wisconsin was that there was always lots of food around the house, something I wasn't used to. There were mornings I woke up at Wayne and Patty's and made an entire package of bacon. I sat and ate the whole thing all by myself—because I could. I loved every minute of it, though I had gone from weighing 118 pounds to 155 pounds pretty quickly. I drank can after can of Mountain Dew and ate boxes of ice cream bars and bags of potato chips. I loved pork barbecue and baked beans. I indulged my every impulse without any thought or awareness that I was putting on so much extra weight. When you're not used to having food readily available, it becomes an obsession when it is.

A 100 GRAND candy bar became my chocolate bar of choice. It represented so much more than chocolate to me. I used to dream of someday making that much money. The dollar figure on the candy wrapper represented financial freedom. It meant wealth and having a rich life. Money meant more to me than just material gain. It was insulation that would allow me to create a fulfilling and meaningful life. And, most important, it meant the kids and I would never have to worry again.

In addition to putting on the extra weight, I had cut my hair into a mullet and got a really bad perm that made my hair frizzy. I looked like a female Billy Ray Cyrus (before he got cute!). Worse yet, I had become more aware that I desperately needed braces to fix my severe overbite and crooked teeth.

Despite my teenage awkwardness Duane always made me feel beautiful. He wrote me extraordinary love letters from basic training, but our relationship was changing with the distance. Shortly after I started my junior year of high school, I boarded a Greyhound bus and made the long two-day trip from Wisconsin to see Duane, who was visiting his father and stepmother in Kalispell, Montana.

I was so excited to see Duane. I stared out the window the entire trip, taking in the beauty of the American landscape that whizzed past me on the two-lane highway. I thought about my life and how much it had changed in such a short period of time. I had been so depressed from not seeing my brothers and sisters for months, and it was good to know I was going to see Duane.

As we got closer to the final stop, I put pink spongy rollers in my hair so I would look fresh and pretty when Duane saw me.

Even though it was late October, it was bitter cold. It was a different type of cold than I was used to growing up in Washington. My trip was extraordinary, and Montana was beautiful.

Duane was just as I had remembered him—handsome, fun, and free-spirited. It was sad when I had to leave him again, but at least it wasn't as traumatic as leaving him in Seattle.

I was comfortable in my new life in Wisconsin and eventually my depression lifted. I was now working, making my own money, and living in a stable and secure home. I had my own room, and my privacy was respected. I decorated the walls with posters of the forests in the Pacific Northwest that reminded me of my trip with Duane. I had the furniture Grandma sent me, which created a pretty, cozy environment.

All alone, on the edge of seventeen.   *Stevie Nicks*

I started listening to a lot of different types of music. It helped me drown out the lonely thoughts I was having from being so far away from the kids. I turned up the music as loud as I could. The louder, the better. I sang along, even though I can't carry a note. Music kept me sane and made me feel whole. I think music is food for your soul. I listened to Journey, Heart, Van Halen, 38 Special, Rush, AC/DC, The Doobie Brothers, and Fleetwood Mac. I loved Steve Perry and Stevie Nicks the most.

I also started reading Danielle Steel novels one after another. I couldn't put her books down. They opened my eyes to a new world. I read them and began daydreaming about what it might be like to someday live a glamorous, exciting, sophisticated life such as the ones strewn throughout the pages of her novels. Danielle Steel's books were romantic and dreamlike, usually revolving around Cinderella-type characters who had fabulous European royal-sounding names.

Me at 9 months.

Cindy with me at 18 months.

Grandma Dicie, shown here in her 20s, was always glamorous.

Grandma Lorraine at 40.

Our cottage on Grant Street in Santa Monica, California.

Grandma Dicie with the actor Tyrone Powers.

Grandma Dicie enjoys the sun.

Grandma Lorraine happy in California, 1942.

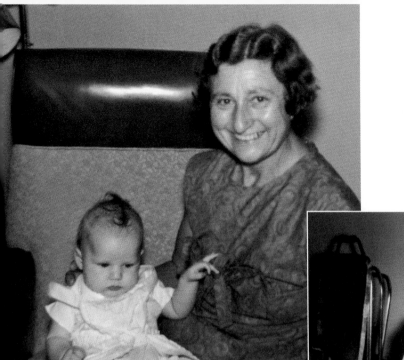

*Grandma Lorraine at 48 and me at
3 months. She was so happy I was a girl.*

*Trying out my vocal
chords. I loved being
loud at 14 months.*

*Cindy and me in our pajamas getting ready for bed at Grandma
Lorraine's house.*

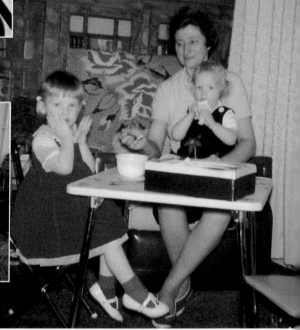

Me at Christmas. I still love Christmas—tons of fun, presents, and toys.

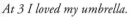

At 3 I loved my umbrella.

Cindy and me in front of Grandma's house dressed for church.

Grandma feeding me in our living room and Cindy enjoying herself in Grandma's lap.

Clockwise, from left: Me, my cousin Tracy, Cindy, and my cousin Trisha, all at Aunt Peggy's house.

Cindy and me on Grandma's porch in 1969, going to Sabbath school.

One of our favorite places—the corner sandbox in Grandma's backyard.

Aunt Betty's 51st birthday in Grandma's dining room, 1969, with Grandma's cream cheese and peach cake, Aunt Betty's favorite.

Cindy and me at 4 and 5.

In Grandma's front yard wearing my dress-up gown and gloves from the Salvation Army store.

Grandma Lorraine at the church bake sale with all her goodies.

Grandma Lorraine's Birthday Cake

1	box (18.25 oz.) yellow cake mix
2	eggs
$\frac{1}{3}$	cup vegetable oil
$\frac{1}{2}$	cup white cranberry juice
$2\frac{1}{2}$	teaspoons raspberry extract
1	can (16 oz.) white frosting
1	pouch (6 oz.) pink writing icings, Wilton
	Flower and letter candy decorations, Wilton
	Candy rainbow sprinkles, Wilton

1. Bake two 8-inch cakes according to package directions, except for the addition of $1\frac{1}{2}$ teaspoons raspberry extract to the batter and substituting the white cranberry juice for the water. Let cakes cool completely. Transfer each cake to an inverted 9-inch pie tin.
2. Add 1 teaspoon extract to frosting and combine thoroughly. Frost each cake. Use a star tip to pipe pink icing around the bottom of each cake where it meets the pie tin. Decorate as desired.

Me at 3 and Cindy at 2 in Grandma's kitchen enjoying our favorite pedestal birthday cakes. My birthday is July 3 and Cindy's is July 7, so we always celebrated together.

Cindy at 3 and me at 4 with our birthday cakes on July 4th weekend.

Cindy at 5 and me at 6 with more cakes.

Cindy and me in our bedroom at Grandma's.

Clockwise: Johnny being held by Cindy with Richie and Kimmy in our living room in Sumner, Washington.

Johnny and me playing.

Kimmy at 7 and me at 13 returning to the Sumner house after a trip to the grocery store.

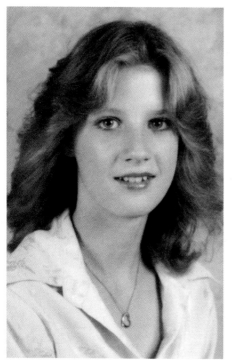

My school picture at 13.

In front of Grandma's house when I was 15 and Cindy was 14.

My high school pom-pom photo, 1983.

Senior photo 1984 in a dress that my friend Mary McCoy made for me.

Just baptized in the Jordan River in Israel. Grandma and I are sitting along the riverbank in the exact place where Jesus was baptized. Grandma was elated!

Colleen and me: girls' night out!

Aunt Peggy and Uncle Bill, Christmas 1988.

*Left to right:
Richie, me,
and Johnny.*

*My Blue Ribbon for Outstanding
Commercial Exhibit in the Los Angeles
County Fair in 1992.*

*Above, right: Kimmy and me on
the road at the Florida State Fair.
Right: At dinner after the close of
the Hawaii Home Show.*

Kurtain Kraft display booth at the Tacoma Holiday and Gift Show in Washington.

Demonstrating Floral Kraft, left, and Kurtain Kraft, below, at QVC in London, England.

Left: The Floral Kraft product line.

Set design: making a topiary tree of moss from a Styrofoam cone.

Stenciling a lampshade.

With my dog, Aspen, at a home show in Los Angeles.

I remember reading about the 21 Club in New York City. Though I had never been there, I could visualize every inch of the place. I could see the colorful jockeys holding up lanterns outside the black wrought-iron gate and taste the famous 21 Club hamburger. I learned about special places in Europe such as Annabelle's in London and The Ritz in Paris from reading Danielle Steel books. Her stories inspired me to someday travel the globe to see the exotic locations she wrote about.

The way Danielle Steel wrote made me want to also become a writer. I started writing for my high school paper. Soon I became the entertainment editor. One of the highlights of that job was getting tickets and a backstage pass to nearly every concert that came to town. I was a legitimate writer, and I took my responsibilities very seriously. I showed off my credentials as if I were a reporter for *The New York Times*.

Danielle Steel's books reminded me of the stories Grandma used to tell me about traveling with Aunt Betty. Her stories of Egypt and Greece seemed as exotic to me as one of Danielle Steel's stories. I shared my daydreams with Grandma Lorraine, telling her how I someday hoped to be like one of Danielle Steel's characters, traveling the world in search of wonderful adventure. She told me her dream was to someday travel to the Holy Land with Cindy and me.

Sometimes dreams do come true because Grandma Lorraine surprised my sister and me with a trip to Egypt, Israel, Turkey, and Greece in 1985. It was a month-long pilgrimage organized through her church. I was so excited to see the historical landmarks from the Bible. Grandma Lorraine wanted us to visit all the places Jesus had been and experience this once-in-a-lifetime trip with her.

Just prior to leaving on our trip, I had oral surgery to correct my overbite. I had worn braces the year before, but I didn't wear my headgear. The orthodontist told me I could either do it all over again or have surgery on my jaw.

After the surgery my jaw was wired shut for the entire trip to the Middle East. I had to eat all of my meals through a straw. While looking for a bathroom in Cairo, I made the mistake of walking into the kitchen in our hotel. I saw the largest cockroaches flying and crawling on every surface. After that, eating in Egypt didn't seem all that important. The outcome from my surgery was a beautiful straight jawline and a much smaller waistline. I lost nearly 30 pounds on that trip and have never put the weight back on.

We arrived in Cairo in the middle of the night. The city was lit up like a beautiful Christmas tree. I could see the pyramids and sphinxes off in the distance. I would have thought the pyramids were farther away from the city, perhaps isolated in the middle of the desert. But they weren't. They are actually very close to the city center. Outside my hotel room I could see the Nile River, which looked like a long, neverending strip of water running across the horizon. By day Cairo was a very dirty city, but at night it looked like a beautiful, serene desert oasis.

We spent the blistering hot June and July days exploring Egypt, climbing the pyramids, visiting the Tomb of the King, and riding camels. From Cairo we visited Israel, where we toured Jerusalem, Masada, and Haifa. I was baptized in the very place that Jesus had been baptized when we visited the Jordan River. Grandma was so elated she could barely contain herself. From Israel we went back through Turkey and then

Greece and the Greek Islands before flying back to the United States. It was an unbelievable trip that I'll never forget for many reasons. Grandma Lorraine fulfilled her lifetime dream, and I was blessed with the gift of being able to share it with her. It was also truly eye-opening for me to see the children in some of these countries. Many of these children had circumstances that were far worse than mine and it made me feel ashamed that I had ever felt sorry for myself.

Chapter Six
Family Shadow

Adversity is the first path to truth.   *Lord Byron*

Three words come to mind when I think about how I felt living in Washington: chaotic, anxious, and terrified. All of those feelings subsided as I got to know myself in Wisconsin.

I began to focus on school. Wayne said I could get my own car if I had a 3.0 grade point average. I was ecstatic because I desperately wanted the opportunity for more freedom. I already knew how to earn my way, making money since I was a little girl. I understood the benefits of hard work. It paid off, and in this case the benefit of getting good grades was a new car.

I got a full-time job the summer between my junior and senior years working in the office at the National Guard Armory near the high school. I walked to and from work every day. I was responsible for organizing everything from paperwork to paper clips. I ran the back supply room like a sergeant, giving it order and structure. I was able to save all of the money I made that summer to put toward the purchase of my car. I was so happy. Life was good.

Toward the end of the summer, I noticed Wayne and Patty were arguing and fighting all the time. I had seen this behavior before. Memories of Vicky and Richard flooded my thoughts. I began to feel anxious and worried about the situation at home. I couldn't believe I was caught in another domestic war.

Wayne continued to drink a lot, but this was the first time he was so volatile that his behavior scared me. I walked in from work one afternoon to find Wayne and Patty screaming at each other in the basement where the master bedroom was. I was tired of their fighting. I'd been through years of this with Vicky and Richard. I thought it was just another meaningless argument, so I left.

The next morning the sheriff came to see me at work. I had no idea why he wanted to talk, but I knew it couldn't be good. He began questioning me about what occurred at home the day before. I told him everything I could remember. I explained Patty and Wayne fought all the time.

The sheriff explained that Patty had filed serious charges against Wayne, claiming domestic violence. I couldn't believe what I was hearing. A few days later Wayne was arrested and taken to jail.

Wayne's trial quickly became the big story in our small town. My name was all over the local paper as the daughter who had walked in on her father's horrific crimes. The media sensationalized every aspect of the story.

I was horrified and completely ashamed as I started my senior year. I could feel all the eyes staring at me when I walked the hallways at school. I heard the whispers shared between the parents when I attended basketball games and pep rallies. I was made co-captain of the pom-pom squad my senior year, something I had wanted to do since I was a little girl.

Although I had tried out twice when I lived in Washington, Vicky found a reason to lash out at me the day before each tryout, leaving me too distraught to make the team. At that time it was impossible for me to smile through my tears. This time, however, I had the strength and courage to stand in the center of the basketball court, cheering away as if nothing was wrong, and somehow compartmentalize what was going on with Wayne and my life. Even though I could hear every word, I pretended I didn't know that the parents were exaggerating and gossiping about the tales that I was certain the media was distorting.

Parents didn't want their children associating with me. I came to Wisconsin to start my life all over, and suddenly it felt as if my carefree life had ended. In an effort to stop the inclusion of my name in the newspaper stories, I went down to the *La Crosse Tribune* and asked to speak to the reporter who had been writing all of the pieces. When I was brought into his office, the look on his face told me he had no idea who I was. I told him that he was ruining my life. I reminded him that I was a minor and that I thought he had no legal right to put my name in the articles. He explained to me that because I was a witness and not the accused, he did in fact have the legal right to use my name. He made it clear that he was not going to stop digging around. I was certain his agenda was to expose a nest of nastiness whether it existed or not. I was furious with him and his justifications made me even angrier.

Wayne didn't want me in the courtroom during the trial except when I had to give my testimony. He was adamant that I not hear the details that other people were going to share when called up on the stand. Wayne never coached me or told me what to say. He told me to tell the truth as I saw it and not to worry about the outcome.

By Christmas Wayne had been convicted and sentenced to two years in jail for second-degree sexual assault. The first time I visited him, he sat on the other side of a thick piece of glass holding a receiver to his ear as we spoke over a two-way phone. I brought him a flannel shirt that Christmas without realizing he couldn't wear it because he had to wear his orange jumper.

I looked at him through the glass and realized that everything Richard and Vicky told me about Wayne over the years must have been true because now he was sitting in jail for committing sickening acts of violence. I was being punished every day at school for his actions as if his conviction was a sentence for me too.

I went to live with a friend for the next few months, but her father was sick and her mother too overwhelmed for me to stay. Grandma got on a plane to visit. This time she suggested I get my own place. She thought I'd be better off since I only had a few months to go before I graduated and turned 18.

We found a great one-bedroom apartment. She signed the lease for me and offered $500 a month to help pay my expenses. I had finally bought my own car, a big brown Dodge Charger with mag wheels and thick black racing stripes on the doors. I could pack a lot of friends in that car. Thank God for those good midwestern girls—they never once made me feel as if I were responsible for my father's crime even though their parents didn't want them to hang around with me.

By the time I got my apartment, one of Wayne's friends, Mary McCoy, who was the head of the La Crosse Department of Unemployment, and I had become friends. She helped me get a job at a local pet store in the mall where I worked every day after school as well as Saturdays and Sundays.

Mary took on a parental role with me and became a mentor. She was one of the strongest and most fabulous women I ever met. She drove an old diesel Mercedes Benz, which I thought was so chic. I loved the sound of the engine, which growled a low "grrrr" sound.

Mary was a single mom working hard to provide great opportunities for her family. She traveled all over the world, which I thought was so Danielle Steel. She was the big sister I never had. I often spent my weekend evenings with Mary and her children having dinner or going to the movies. She represented everything Vicky was not. People respected and admired Mary. She kept me grounded, inspiring me to do great things with my life. She showed me that women could be smart, work, raise a family, and make a difference in the world, their community, and even the life of one young girl who admired an older, wiser teacher.

Mary taught me how to show compassion to those people in the world who are less fortunate. Like Grandma she led by example, teaching me to be more thoughtful about bigger issues than my own. I knew I could apply her lessons to my own life. I was so used to most adults being completely self-absorbed, not selfless like Mary.

Mary and Grandma Lorraine spoke often, especially after Wayne was sent to jail. Mary looked out for me through the end of my senior year of high school because she worried about me being on my own.

When I didn't have a date for the senior prom, Mary suggested I have dinner with a girlfriend so I didn't sit home alone in my apartment. She even made me a mauve V-neck dress that fell just below the knee. It tied at the waist with an embroidered sash, which really made the dress special. Mary also made my graduation dress. It was a beautiful, light green, with delicate lace details and pearl white buttons.

I always knew I could count on Mary for anything and everything I needed. It was comforting to know that someone cared and was always available for me.

Chapter Seven
On My Own

Destiny is not a matter of chance, it is a matter of choice; it is not a thing to be waited for, it is a thing to be achieved.
William Jennings Bryan, Congressman, 1899

After graduating high school I thought about becoming a physical therapist. The University of Wisconsin-La Crosse had one of the best programs in the state, so there was no reason to leave the area. I moved from the apartment Grandma Lorraine got me to another apartment the summer before college. I roomed with a girlfriend whose name was also Sandra. We had a two-bedroom apartment on the north side of town. Our main goal that summer was to have fun.

I was eager to start fresh. My senior year in high school had been overshadowed by the headlines of Wayne's arrest, trial, and conviction. I couldn't escape the press of being his daughter. Going to college was a perfect opportunity to reinvent myself. It was like starting all over again with a clean slate.

I didn't have to be Wayne and Vicky's daughter anymore. I could become my own person. I enjoyed discovering what I liked all by myself without any other pressures or influences. The choices were mine to make.

I spent that summer before my freshman year of college socializing and going to parties. I had become more carefree than I ever thought possible. Duane and I had broken up by the end of my senior year in high school. The distance and disconnect had taken its toll and we were both on to our new lives. There would be no A-frame on the Oregon coastline. There would be no children. At this point in my life, that was fine with me.

I had a new boyfriend named Mike, who at first was as fun and carefree as I had planned my summer to be. But I soon discovered that he was controlling and quick tempered. One night in mid-July, I went out with my girlfriends, whooping it up in downtown La Crosse. Mike and I hadn't planned on meeting up that evening—it was a girls' night out. I would normally call him when I got home, but on this night it was too late and I didn't want to wake him.

I climbed into bed around 2 a.m., happy to have the comfort of my soft pillow and cool white sheets. The next morning I heard my bedroom door open and could sense it was Mike. I rolled over and looked up at him, happy that he had come by to wake me up. I was shocked when his clenched fist hit me right on the side of my face.

Thwack!

He was livid that I had stayed out so late and didn't call. He was in a jealous rage.

I sprang out of bed like a cartoon character, picked up my portable telephone that was next to the bed, and started hitting him right back. I was furious that he had struck me. He took the brunt of a full-blown retaliation for all that had been wrong in my life. Before I realized it I was standing over Mike as he crouched down in a corner of my kitchen.

"Get out!" I yelled at him.

I jumped into my car and drove to his parents' house. I had become close to his mother and wanted her to see what her son had done. By the time I got to her home, my eye was almost swollen shut. I don't know what I expected when I got there, but I figured that she would be sympathetic when she saw me. To my surprise she didn't acknowledge my injury at all. Mike had told me that his mother had been a victim of abuse. I could only guess her lack of reaction when seeing me was from her own experiences.

Needless to say, Mike and I broke up. I was never going to allow myself to be in an abusive relationship. I had seen what it did to Vicky and Patty. I was not going to end up like them.

After the breakup I really wanted to just be free. It was my summer to be irresponsible. I was late with my rent check more than once. I wasn't managing my bank account and bounced a check. I was continually late for work and ended up losing my job at the pet store. What surprised me most about being fired was that I didn't feel bad—it was actually a relief. I felt great because I didn't have any responsibilities, no one to answer to, and nowhere I had to be. I wanted to have one summer for myself. I had the ability to do whatever I wanted, including making mistakes.

I ran through my savings quickly, and before I knew it the money was gone. The thought of having to call Grandma Lorraine to ask for more was something I just couldn't bear. I knew I needed help fast and thought that maybe Richard would do something supportive and nice for me now. Since he hadn't been helpful in the past, I was hoping that enough time had gone by that he would have realized the sacrifices I made to help out at home when I lived in Washington. Certainly that had some value to him.

I felt desperate, so I picked up the phone and called him to ask for the money. Surprisingly he was patient and calm on the phone, listening to what I was saying. I thought he might actually help me this one time. He said he would think about what I had shared and find a way to make it all right. I was grateful.

Shortly thereafter I received a letter from Richard. When I pulled it from the mailbox, relief washed over me. I knew there would be a check inside and that this would be his way to show me that he cared. He was finally going to save the day. I was so happy that I had called and happier still that he was going to step up and do what he could to make things right. I ripped open the letter and found no check. There was just a long explanation spanning page after page of how concerned he was that I was making a mess of my life, overspending money while being "flip" and "thoughtless." He had turned my request for helping me out of a financial bind into a request for luxurious indulgences, such as new furniture and a stereo, when I needed money for rent and food.

Only pure desperation allowed me to even consider reaching out to Vicky. I hated needing to ask her for anything, but I felt I had nowhere else to turn. I finally made the call and, to my surprise, she asked no questions. She said she'd send me a check. When I got it in the mail, I immediately deposited it into my account.

I don't remember exactly how much the check was for, but I do recall that the check bounced.

The landslide of financial repercussions that followed caused me tremendous anxiety and stress. All of the checks I wrote against that deposit bounced, and the service charges I incurred for the returned checks were astronomical. I was left even further in debt than I was before I asked for Vicky's help.

Richard's letter and Vicky's bounced check snapped me back into reality and right out of my summer of fun.

Childhood trauma and suffering does not provide us with an excuse for our problems. It explains the origins of our problems while in no way relieving us of the responsibility to understand and improve ourselves.

Peter R. Breggin, M.D.,
The Heart of Being Helpful: Empathy and the Creation of a Healing Presence

I realized that I had the potential to mess up my life even worse than Vicky. It was a seminal moment in which I fully understood the consequences of my own poor choices and bad behavior. Most important, I knew I was an adult and the only person responsible for keeping my life together. I wanted to have a better life than what I had known. Those thoughts and Richard's letter had set me on a straight course. In Richard's final fatherly denial, he had inadvertently given me the best gift of all. He opened my eyes wide and clear and destroyed any notion I still had of receiving support from a parent. It was time to live my best life completely on my own.

For the rest of the summer, I found a better job working at a very chic and expensive women's clothing store called the Dahl House. I idolized the women who worked there, especially the woman who ran the store because she was so lovely to me. She taught me how to run the cash register, work the computer, and basically showed me the ropes. Working at that store exposed me to some of the finer things in life. I had no idea women would pay so much money for clothes!

There was one woman who worked at the store who was very snooty. She was married to a doctor and I felt as if she always looked down her nose at me, as if I wasn't good enough to be working in the same store with her. She was thin, blond, pretty, and looked more like one of our customers than a saleswoman.

She had impeccable taste. I could hardly wait to see her home when she invited all five employees of the store for a small holiday party. Everything was so neat! There was no clutter at all on the kitchen counters or any other visible surface for that matter! There were no papers stacked up, old magazines in a pile, nothing!

She had pretty, fragrant candles lit everywhere, potpourri in a sterling silver bowl, and monogrammed hand towels next to the sink in the powder room. Her home was calm and peaceful. It was perfect right down to the roaring fire in the stone fireplace and the classical music playing from the built-in ceiling speakers. It was so "grown up."

There were no children—never had been and never would be. She was pretty uptight and structured. The very thought of kids running around her perfect home must have been terrifying to her, I'm sure. I left that evening realizing I had never been in such a lovely house. It was wonderful, clean, and organized. And although she was never nice to me, it was an eye-opening experience to see how she lived.

Unknowingly she inspired me to strive for a higher standard of living. I was really drawn to the calm and serenity I felt that night. I liked the finishings and fabrics. I knew what the finer things looked like, but I hadn't many opportunities to experience them firsthand. I knew I had a flair for making fabric drape well and for matching colors.

When I was a little girl, some of the very best days of my life were when the JCPenney and Sears catalogs would arrive. That was Toyland for me. I tore out pages of clothing and planned my dream wardrobe, if only I had the money. I ripped out bedroom sets I liked and amazing bath and bed linens. I chose comforters and sheets, towels and rugs. I was always designing, planning, mixing, and matching. This was the life I dreamed of. It was the life I knew I would someday have.

Seeing my coworker's house taught me something very valuable that I will never forget. Despite all its beauty and elegance, it didn't feel like a home. It lacked warmth, comfort, and love.

Freshman year was the beginning of a new life. I alone was responsible for my success or failure. I took the basic classes along with a couple of business courses during the first semester. I excelled in accounting and marketing classes as well as in English. I knew those classes would someday come in handy!

When the time came to declare a major, my heart wasn't into physical therapy and I decided to pursue a business degree. Many of the classes I wanted to take were already filled, but I attended them anyway. I knew if someone fell out of the class, I would be the first person to take his or her place. By the time tests were given, the professors didn't know I wasn't supposed to be in the class, so I usually was able to remain for the semester.

Business management and marketing were by far my favorite subjects. I had a knack for putting together business outlines and marketing plans. I researched various ideas, studied business models, and continued to advance my studies through practical application of those plans outside the classroom. One of my classes required me to start a mock retail business. I chose a pizzeria and ice cream shop as my start-up. There was a local pizza place I liked called Rocky Rococo's and a sandwich shop called Lindy's that were very popular at the time, so I decided to combine the two ideas into one location as my project. I had to find a mock storefront, hire contractors to build out the space, and do a financial analysis and feasibility study of the business—initial financial investment, three years of profit and loss projections with detailed accounting, and accounts payable and receivable listings, along with an outline of competitors and possible investors. In other words, I had to compile everything it would take to start a business.

It was an amazing amount of work, but it taught me valuable lessons I have never forgotten. What I learned in these classes, especially this project, was the most important thing I learned in college because it taught me how to focus on a single project and think through every aspect from beginning to end. It made me feel as if I was really going to be able to implement a successful business plan, skills I use to this day.

In addition to my classes, I changed jobs and began working as a waitress at the Ramada Inn in the mornings for breakfast hours. After my shift I went to class. I served lunch two days a week at a local Chinese restaurant and went back to class in the afternoons. At night I went back to the Ramada Inn to cocktail waitress. Occasionally I got to bartend. I really had that schedule down!

Shortly after I started college, I met a great guy named Brit who also was a student at La Crosse. He was cute, sweet, and fun—perfect boyfriend material for me. One night he took me to a party and introduced me to a group of other students that he had gone to high school with. One of the girls in the group really stood out. Her name was Colleen. She was beautiful, dynamic, and had a quick wit. She was irreverently sarcastic, had great style, and a sassy spirit. She was tall, blond, and clearly the most popular in the group. I knew some of the girls in the group from the college pom-pom squad I had just tried out for and much to my surprise had made. Colleen and I instantly became friends.

She had been crowned Snow Queen in Westby, Wisconsin, a year or so before we met. The Snow Queen is named during the annual international ski jumping competition. Almost every girl in the small towns around Westby grows up dreaming of becoming the Snow Queen. It was more prestigious and important than being prom queen.

"Finally!" I thought. "I get to have some fun!"

Colleen came from a great family. She was raised in a happy home, and it showed in everything she did.

As the year went on, we were inseparable. We became best friends and remain so to this day. We have been through everything together—marriages, kids, breakups, divorce, deaths, and every other life lesson two best friends can share.

In college none of those issues had surfaced yet. We were just two girls having fun! I had a great job and a car, and I now lived across from campus. I wasn't in contact with Wayne or Vicky. Grandma Lorraine was still sending me money every month. Colleen was dating Tim, the college football star who was blond and drop-dead gorgeous. I was still dating Brit, so life was pretty good.

At the start of my sophomore year, I was happily living with five other girls. Our house was next to a big sorority on Main Street, so there were always a lot of students and friends around. My room was a porch that had been converted into a beautiful bedroom. I put up gorgeous floral curtains and had a double-pedestal water bed that had doors and drawers on the lower section. I vividly remember buying the water bed for $349.95 complete with delivery and installation! While that may not sound like a lot of money today, it may as well have been $5,000 because it was all the same to me back then.

I had a matching double dresser and nightstands on either side of the bed. I hung an ornate plastic gold-painted mirror and strung tiny white holiday lights around the perimeter of the room giving it a soft, warm glow at night. It was a perfect place to come back to after a fun night out with friends!

By this time I had taken out a bunch of student loans and bought a shiny black Pontiac Fiero. I was working two jobs and going to school. My best friend seemed like the most popular girl on campus, and I was having the time of my life. The only things I had to deal with were school, work, and pom-pom practice. I was feeling really good, getting good grades, and enjoying every moment.

As amazing as things were in my life, my sister Kimmy was having a really difficult time back in Washington. She wasn't getting along with Richard and wanted to come visit me at school. I hadn't seen her in quite some time, so I was thrilled. When she came to see me, she told me she wanted to tell Richard off because he was being a strict disciplinarian, something I was not when I was living at home taking care of the kids. It was typical teenage angst, which felt magnified because she hadn't any parental structure from an adult until she lived with Richard.

I had planned to go back to Washington for Christmas to see all of the kids. I was really looking forward to that trip. Richard's new wife, Gloria, was a very calming influence. She brought structure and order into their lives, created a real home for them, and demonstrated her love and support for the kids. She had given up a life of luxury, her beautiful house on a lake, and a sports car to mother these children who weren't her own but who clearly needed her. She also created an environment that made it tolerable for me to be in a room with Richard.

When Kimmy visited me and explained her frustration, I reminded her of Gloria and the sacrifices she had made for her and my brothers. I tried to dissuade Kimmy from making a big deal out of her situation, telling her it was completely normal to feel the way she did and even reminding her that things could be a lot worse—she could still be living with Vicky.

We often received crank calls at the house where I was living at the time. One day after Kimmy left, a boyfriend of one of my roommates answered the phone, thinking it was a crank caller. He said, "Listen, you jerk! If you call here again, I'm going to come find you and beat the crap out of you!" We were all standing there wide-eyed, thrilled with his threat, and hopeful the calls would now stop. Then I noticed a strange look on his face. He handed me the phone and said, "It's for you."

My heart was pounding because his look told me something terrible had happened. I thought someone had died. When I said hello I heard Richard's voice on the other end. Although I don't remember his exact words, he said something to the effect of, "I know how messed up you are and what you have done to your sister. She came home and told me off, and you put her up to it. You are no longer welcome in my home or this family." He hung up before I could say a word.

With one call Richard had disowned me. After everything I'd been through, he was going to take away my siblings forever. I couldn't believe what I was hearing from this man. It was the last straw. With tears streaming down my face, I put down the receiver and washed my hands of him from that day on. I spent Christmas with Brit and his family.

At the end of my sophomore year, Colleen told me she and Tim were getting married. After she graduated in December, they planned to move from La Crosse to Milwaukee. How would I survive without Colleen? Because of Richard I hadn't spoken to the kids in months, but Colleen had been my security blanket—my best friend—and now she was leaving. I couldn't stay in school without her.

That summer I broke up with Brit and decided to take a road trip with one of my other college friends, Ann. We drove from Wisconsin to California and had the time of our lives touring and meeting new people along the way. We zigzagged from Lake Tahoe to Los Angeles and back through Arizona before making the trip home to Wisconsin.

When I got back to La Crosse, I knew for sure that life at school without my best friend would be too lonely to bear. I loved California and decided that I would move there when Colleen graduated in December 1987.

Earlier in the year Uncle Bill and Aunt Peggy had stopped in La Crosse to visit me while on one of their many road trips across America. They insisted I come live with them in California. They didn't understand how I survived in the cold and snow! I thought about their offer and knew it could be a great change of pace. It made a lot of sense to move back to California so I could be closer to Grandma Lorraine, Uncle Bill, and Aunt Peggy, which is where I felt I truly belonged.

I called Aunt Peggy and Uncle Bill to let them know I was accepting their offer. I flew to Los Angeles for Thanksgiving to see if I could line up a job in advance. I interviewed at a Denny's restaurant near my aunt and uncle's home in the valley. Denny's offered me a management position on the spot with a starting salary of $50,000 a year! The money was awfully appealing. I also interviewed at CJ's, a clothing store in Pacific Palisades. Even though it was an hour-and-fifteen-minute commute each way, I really wanted that job. They also offered me a management position, which I was excited to accept. I had secured full-time employment for when I came back to Los Angeles in a few weeks.

I left college in the middle of my junior year and never went back. By January 1988 I was working full time at the clothing store and trying to settle into a new life. Everything had come full circle and I was back home.

Chapter Eight
Because I Didn't Know I Couldn't

What we learn to do we learn by doing.   *Aristotle*

Not long after arriving at Aunt Peggy and Uncle Bill's, I moved into a house in Malibu where I rented a single room so I could be closer to work. I decorated my room using billowing pink shearing fabric that I bought for next to nothing at a warehouse in downtown Los Angeles. I used old coat hangers to create hooks and loops that I wove fabric around and through to give it movement, depth, shape, and pizzazz. I'd wire the fabric into a curtain rod to create stunning valances. Everyone who saw my creation loved what I had done and it was so easy to do. I always made all my bedrooms look special by decorating with fabric, even my apartments in college.

When Uncle Bill saw my invention, he thought it was fabulous. He told me I should sell my product and recommended I find someone to weld my mocked-up prototypes together. Although he fully believed I was on to something big, I didn't take him seriously at the time. I thought my uncle was just being kind and complimentary, but it turned out friends were asking me to come to their homes to work my window magic on a pretty regular basis.

Shortly after I got to California, the clothing store I was working at closed. I wanted to stay in Malibu, so I found a new job working for an import-export company. The owner, Zane, was also a local attorney with a thriving law practice. I was hired to help run his offices. I did everything from accounts payable to accounts receivable, logging orders for product sales, and placing orders overseas for products being imported.

My presence in Zane's office allowed him to focus on his clients who needed his legal services. Zane's primary import business was made up of personal protection devices such as stun guns and home security systems including doorknob alarms.

In addition to working for Zane, I started working nights as a bartender and cocktail waitress at the Malibu Adobe, a popular restaurant that was one of the favorite hot spots for celebrities and socialites in Malibu. While I was working there, I was told the restaurant had been decorated by Ali MacGraw and was co-owned by Michael Landon. Both superstars came in from time to time.

The restaurant was white stucco adobe style, with gorgeous round, bleached beams exposed across the ceiling and a large outdoor patio in the front. It looked as if it should have been in Santa Fe, New Mexico, not in Malibu, California, two blocks east of the ocean.

It was a very friendly atmosphere. It had an almost magical feel because the people who came in were all hip, happening young and old Hollywood stars out for a good time.

It was common to see many celebrities hanging out on any given night. All the members of Hollywood's Brat Pack came in on a regular basis, including Demi Moore, Charlie Sheen, Emilio Estevez, and Molly Ringwald. I couldn't believe how lucky I was to be working in one of the most famous restaurants in Malibu, serving the stars I only saw in movies back in Wisconsin.

One night Charlie Sheen came into the restaurant as I was working the patio area. He noticed a rather large tough guy giving me a hard time. It wasn't unusual for some of the patrons to harass the waitresses. It was obvious this guy had had too much to drink. He was slurring his words and being aggressive every time I walked by with a full tray of drinks. I had gotten pretty good at the bob and weave every cocktail waitress relies on to navigate a crowded bar. But this guy was truly testing my patience and challenging my dodging technique. He was becoming more aggressive than I was comfortable with, but there wasn't much I could do about it.

Sensing my discomfort Charlie Sheen walked up to where I was standing, put his arm around me, and told the drunken guy I was his girlfriend. I could see fear wash over the drunken guy's face at the thought that he just insulted Charlie Sheen's girlfriend. I nearly burst out laughing because the guy was dumbfounded and backed off immediately. Of course I didn't really know Charlie other than to serve him a few drinks during the year or so that I had worked there. He ordered a Coke from me, paid for his drink, and gave me a $20 tip!

Even though I had two pretty good jobs, I was having a hard time making enough money to pay off my student loans, which hung very heavy over my head. One afternoon Zane came to me and asked me if I wanted to start working trade shows for him, selling the products that he imported. He thought it was a good way to help me earn some much-needed extra money and an awesome new outlet for his products. He agreed to front the costs of all of the products if I could arrange and pay for a booth at the Del Mar County Fair, north of San Diego. Zane told me I could pay him back the wholesale cost of the products out of the money I would make from the show and that I could keep the rest.

I called the organizers of the fair to see if there was any space available. It was short notice, so I wasn't sure it was even possible. I was told they were completely booked, but if someone cancelled, I would be the first person on the waiting list.

A few days later, I received a call that someone had backed out of a 10x10 in line space. "In line" meant I would be in a small booth located somewhere between two corners. The corner booths were favored because of the additional foot traffic. Beggars can't be choosers, so I grabbed the space.

The only way I could pay for the space was to sell my car. The Fiero sold for $3,800, covering the expense of the booth and leaving me just enough money to pay for a motel and rent a van.

I enlisted the help of my sister Kimmy, and we worked that fair every day for three weeks. We put in 16-hour days and were exhausted by the end of the run but all our hard work and perseverance had really paid off. We made enough money from that show to buy space at three more upcoming fairs and pay off all of my student loans. It was a gift and relief to have that heavy financial burden lifted once and for all.

Living in Malibu became too expensive, so I moved back into my aunt and uncle's house in the San Fernando Valley as a way to save money. I was starting a new business that required all of my profits to be rolled into my venture. I had overhead and needed to keep the business growing. I even had to buy a white cargo van to shuttle my entire inventory from show to show. It wasn't fun like my Fiero, but it definitely served its purpose.

My schedule was keeping me very busy, but I still made time for a social life. I had many new friends, one of whom worked at Western Costume, one of the largest film and television costume suppliers in the world. It is a very famous landmark in Los Angeles. Their warehouse is a virtual archive of Hollywood history. There is a special section in the warehouse called the "Lockup" where the most important costumes are kept under lock and key. It's where you would find dresses from *Gone with the Wind* or Yul Brynner's outfit from *The King and I* and many other all-time-great Hollywood epic films.

Every other year my friend's boss got a call from the members of Fleetwood Mac to help outfit them for their Halloween party. This year, as a token of the band's appreciation, they invited my friend and his boss to the party, which was being held at Christine McVie's house. I was deliriously happy to be included because I knew this would be my chance to meet Stevie Nicks, whom I had loved and adored since high school.

I wore the prettiest period dress I could find in the costume house. Billy Idol was the first person I saw when I walked through the door. Even though it was a costume party, he wore jeans, a T-shirt, and glasses. He had the most beautiful skin and hair. I truly wasn't a big fan until I saw him in person. We spoke for a few minutes, and I thought he was utterly charming. As I turned to walk away, Mick Fleetwood was standing right in front of me. He was so tall and his blazing eyes were absolutely mesmerizing.

The minute I looked at him I found myself a little scared by his daunting presence. The room was filled with lots of familiar faces, including Peter Frampton and Christine McVie.

I've always been the kind of person who stands back and observes the action at a party. I'm usually somewhere on the fringe of the room taking it all in. But here I was in the middle of the mix. I suddenly caught a glimpse of Stevie Nicks who was dressed as Scarlett from *Gone with the Wind*. I knew it was a big deal for her to be wearing that dress. I was in awe. This was the woman who got me through my roughest years growing up. Her album *Bella Donna* was my anthem album through high school and college. I overheard her speaking with a cute young guy who said he was a personal trainer. She decided to take him on tour with her on the spot.

A few moments later I was talking to my friend when someone suddenly came crashing into the back of me. I'm not sure what happened. When I turned around, I cringed. It was Stevie Nicks. I didn't know what to do. She touched me softly on the shoulder and asked if I was all right. She was so lovely and kind. I spent the rest of the night completely amazed and wide-eyed that I was even in the same room with people whose music made my high school years tolerable.

Now I was in control in my life. I was working hard and was now doing things I could only have dreamed about. Being around these people really inspired me to want to do great things with my own life.

I cut back my hours working for Zane and began exhibiting and selling products full time at various home shows and county fairs. By midfall I was exhausted. I came down with a terrible flu the last weekend of the Los Angeles Home Show, so I asked a friend to fill in for me. I was in bed with a virus that knocked me on my back when I received a frantic call. My friend said she was being kicked out of the show for selling stun guns. Even though I was sick as a dog, I threw on a denim dress, pulled my hair back into a ponytail, and put on dark sunglasses. I got into my van and drove one hour to the fairgrounds to see if I could figure out a way to stay in the show.

When I got to the booth, I asked my friend who had kicked us out. She told me the head guy from the show promotion offices shut us down. I couldn't afford what was happening. I needed that money!

I wasn't expecting a young and charming guy just slightly older than me to appear. He looked me up and down, trying to disarm me with kindness, but I wasn't having it. I was sick, irritated, and not into his flirting.

I shook his hand, hoping I would give him the flu. I thought he deserved whatever bug I had. He introduced himself as Dan.

We went for a walk up and down the aisles of the show. He talked nonstop about the show circuit and how it works. I'm not sure if he knew I was new to the business or if he just liked hearing the sound of his own voice. It didn't seem as if he'd ever stop talking. I was feeling nauseous and ready to vomit. Apparently he noticed my green color because he opened an outside door for some fresh air.

He said, "Step into my office."

I don't know why that line tickled me so much, but it did. As if the whole outdoors was his office! He certainly had a big enough ego.

Dan warned me that there was a large liability for selling stun guns at shows because lots of children come with their parents. He was concerned that any of the kids might accidentally hurt themselves. He suggested quietly selling them as a nonadvertised item to protect my interests. Dan agreed to let me keep the booth but made me promise to be more thoughtful about how I displayed the stun guns. He suggested I place them in the back, beyond the reach of a curious child.

The young do not know enough to be prudent, and therefore they attempt the impossible—and achieve it, generation after generation.   *Pearl S. Buck*

I thanked Dan for his concern and assured him I would be careful. Dan and I became best friends, much like my neighbor Mark growing up. He helped me learn the trade show business, advising me on how to navigate, which shows to book, who the good promoters were, and what fairs were worthy of the fee. He mentored me through the early stages of my business.

Another big break came at that same show. I met a representative from Black & Decker who was also selling home security systems. He told me his company was giving up their booths where they promoted and sold do-it-yourself home security systems in all of the national and important state fairs and home shows. It was an opportunity to create more business if they were interested in having me represent their home security product line. I offered to sell their systems nationwide if they could provide Black & Decker booth display units and signage. Combining the Black & Decker line with my already existing products meant success and brand credibility.

Black & Decker trusted me to communicate their brand. I studied the products and learned the installation process and techniques to sell their security systems in every market. Since Black & Decker was already booked in many of the places I wanted to secure booth space, all I had to do was take over their contracts and pay for the space. The association with Black & Decker gave me a bigger and more professional presence than I could have ever had on my own.

Chapter Nine
Creating Kurtain Kraft

The most powerful weapon on earth is the human soul on fire.
Marshal Foch

I worked the shows and state fairs carrying Black & Decker products for about a year. By the summer of 1992, I began to take notice of what other people were selling too. I loved to walk around the home shows, checking out beautiful decorating products. There were so many items I thought I could make on my own. One in particular was a window treatment product that was easy to use at home. I could never understand why anyone paid to have someone hang curtains! I had a unique talent to make any window look fabulous for very little money. I instinctively knew how to hang fabric, giving every room a warmer, richer look, and I loved doing it.

After seeing that product at the trade show, I began to re-think what Uncle Bill had said. Maybe he was right. What if other people liked my invention as much as he did? I wasn't convinced, but it was worth a try. I began working on the products, creating crowns, rings, and lattices. I developed three

112

different ring sizes and turned the lattice into a wreath by re-shaping it and connecting the ends.

Once all the products were pulled together, it was time to figure out the marketing. First order of business was naming the new company. I went with Kurtain Kraft because I was selling curtains as a craft. The "C"s were swapped for "K"s to make the name stand out. The next step was to create a logo and begin branding the new company.

I had trade shows and state fairs already set up, so it was a no-brainer to launch the products in those venues. I had a good reputation and excellent contacts. My business relied on quality relationships as much as it did on the quantity of my contacts. I had those two key elements locked down. I was also enjoying my new on-the-road lifestyle.

Home decorating was meaningful to me because it was always something I loved doing. Grandma always taught me that a house had four walls but that a home reflected its owner. I had a passion for making a room look beautiful and a flair for doing it on a budget. I wasn't sure if my ideas would work, but I'd never know unless I took a chance.

I had 100 of each of my new products made, which was all I could afford at the time. I had booked the Los Angeles County Fair to sell the home security products, so the booth space was already secured. All that I needed to do was rearrange the products and create a new display to accommodate the home decorating line. I had a collapsible metal-frame booth made that was 20 feet across and 10 feet deep. The front portion of the booth would demonstrate to potential customers how easy the decorating products were to install.

I used several types of fabric to demonstrate the different designs on the metal frame of the booth. The Waverly fabric line had the most beautiful designs. It was chintz, and the outcome was always the same—puffy, billowy, and perfect. I had a variety of their designs for the customers to choose from, so they could select their own look and instantly see the finished treatments. The displays gave the illusion of real windows. The booth was awesome. Uncle Bill helped pull it all together, and Kimmy helped sell.

Uncle Bill's hunch was right on. We ran out of product the first weekend. Women were actually bidding on the last few pairs in stock. It was like a half-off sale at the Bon Marché. I had never seen anything like the frenzy over these products. It was a product they never knew they couldn't live without until they saw my demonstrations. It was amazing to see so many women delighted by my creation. Many times women would share their own ideas on how they were going to use the curtain hardware. I loved hearing all of their thoughts. It made me feel proud to have created something so useful.

I had to beg and plead with the welder to stay at work after hours to manufacture more hardware. I didn't have the same profit margins as in home security, but I was moving so much volume that it more than made up for the deficit.

Much to my surprise we won the blue ribbon for booth design and display as well as for best new product. I was definitely onto something big. I never intended to transition out of home security products. It just happened. I originally believed I would have two booths at every show to sell both Black & Decker and Kurtain Kraft. But Kurtain Kraft quickly took over my life.

Selling Kurtain Kraft was so much easier than selling home security systems. There were no liability issues with show managers, no possible accidents, and it required minimal training to sell. I was offering something that the majority of customers previously believed they had to pay thousands of dollars to have professionals install. I was providing them the same look for $19.99 to $39.99 complete.

The business began to grow very quickly, and before I knew it Kurtain Kraft was fast becoming a household name. I invested in the company and nurtured it. I cut my teeth on learning every aspect of building a business. By our third trade show, we were grossing $60,000 a weekend!

Kimmy and I would go back to our hotel room and line up the cash on the bed to count it, putting it into piles divided by denomination. Then we took out the checks and credit card slips and added those up. We stared at our profits for hours. There were times I walked through airports carrying $100,000 in cash and checks. It was unbelievable. Sometimes we'd stop to buy 100 GRAND candy bars in the airport because it was a funny irony and still my favorite chocolate treat. But now that candy bar had a totally different meaning.

Thankfully I was experienced enough in trade shows to understand there is a cost of doing business. I rolled most of the profits right back into the company, investing and developing as we went along.

Kimmy and I brainstormed on ways to build the new business. I started to write a business plan for Kurtain Kraft and mapped out a schedule for upcoming shows. We realized we could double our revenue if we split up, so Kimmy worked one show while I worked another.

I knew I had to package the product to properly launch it in retail. Prior to this decision it was shipped loose in bulk, packed in corrugated boxes. There was literally no retail packaging until I started selling product at Wal-Mart. I asked a good friend named Annie George to help.

Annie had a small design firm that could take on speculative business that larger firms would turn away. She is very talented and creative. Annie, along with her fabulous team, agreed to help design all of the packaging so we could test the retail market. We all worked into the wee hours of the morning trying to come up with something that was simple yet appealing. I thought it would be a slam dunk because I had been so successful selling directly to the consumer.

Boy, was I wrong!

Every retailer told me the same thing. I did not have a demonstration video nor did I have adequate instructions that would teach consumers how to install and use the curtain hardware at home.

They were right.

I spent the next several months creating retail-appropriate instructional videos and printed directions complete with diagrams to be included in the packaging.

Swayed, but not discouraged, I kept working the fairs and trade shows for the rest of 1992 and most of 1993. It was a grueling schedule. Even though I attended shows primarily on weekends, the days were long, usually 12 hours of standing on hard concrete surfaces, talking to customers, and building the business. If I left the booth for 15 minutes to go to the bathroom or eat a hamburger, it translated into a minimum loss of several hundred dollars. There was very little incentive to leave the booth. I either really, really had to go, or I had to be very, very hungry!

While working the Philadelphia Home Show, I was approached by an infomercial producer who loved the products. He offered to do a Kurtain Kraft infomercial and assured me that I wouldn't have to put up any money. He thought it was very possible to make millions of dollars. It sounded too good to be true, but I heard him out anyway. An unexpected call from their largest competitor came shortly after.

A dream is the bearer of a new possibility, the enlarged horizon, the great hope.

Howard Thurman

The success of Kurtain Kraft and its popularity with consumers was spreading like wildfire, but everything I had heard about infomercials led me to believe there would be nothing left for me if I signed away the rights. Although I knew an infomercial was exactly what was needed to take the company to the next level, I wanted to do it on my own.

Kimmy and I worked every fair and show on the circuit. Each of us hired an assistant, and at busier shows we sometimes had two. I spent my weeks ordering more products, booking shows, organizing travel, and running the company. I was 25 years old, traveling all over the country, and making loads of money. Kurtain Kraft had gotten unbelievably popular in a very short period of time. Maybe the success came so quickly because I didn't think I couldn't and perhaps because I had nothing to lose.

One of the great things about having very little guidance when I was growing up and when I was starting my company was that there was nobody to doubt my abilities or second-guess my decisions. Nobody planted the seed of fear that I could fail. That was the first time I realized things that happened in my childhood were finally working for me—not against me. I wasn't afraid. I felt empowered and independent.

With my newfound success I spoiled myself by renting a new apartment in Marina del Rey. It was my first home of my own—no roommates. Living there was one of the happiest times of my life. It was on the 12th floor of the Kingswood apartment complex overlooking Santa Monica. On one side I had a picturesque view of the ocean and the Santa Monica pier. On the other there was the marina with all the beautiful boats in the harbor. It had a gorgeous patio, which I decorated with antique wicker furniture and oversize pillows that were custom-made to fit the furniture. I used a rustic 9-foot wrought-iron gate I found at a secondhand shop as a headboard. It was huge and ornate. I dolled it up by spraying it with gold paint, then wrapped peach silk around the gate, making a canopy out of the fabric.

I decorated the living room with a large white overstuffed couch that was so big that it didn't fit through the door. Uncle Bill had to ask a buddy of his to borrow a crane so he could lift the sofa over the balcony to get it into the apartment. At this point in my life, there were very few things I couldn't deal with calmly and rationally. But getting that couch into my living room was more than I could handle because I was having my housewarming party that very night. The caterer was already in the kitchen and there was no place for anyone to sit! Somehow I forgot to measure the dimensions of the door when I fell in love with the couch and ordered it on the spot. It was a mistake I would never make again!

Thank God for Uncle Bill. With a simple wave of his hand he hoisted the monster sofa up 12 stories and saved my day!

By this time I had saved $50,000 from the shows I'd been doing. Despite the high cost of paying for booth space, some up to nine months in advance, I was able to carve out cash for a rainy day. It was only a matter of time before I had to roll the dice and gamble on doing a Kurtain Kraft infomercial.

I found a television producer who had never done an infomercial but who I could afford. The next step was to cast the various roles. I had never been on camera before, nor did I feel the need to be. I thought I was too young to be taken seriously as a home decorating expert, so I hired C. C. Carr and Leanne Nelson. They were two fabulous women who reminded me of Aunt Peggy and best represented the people who were buying my products at the trade shows.

The key traits I looked for in casting the leads were sincerity and credibility. They had to communicate the product in a way that didn't intimidate the buyer. Because our budget was so small, we shot the entire project on two consecutive nights at the home of the producer's mother-in-law. It was a terrific location because his mother-in-law was a real decorator, so her home was lovely, camera friendly, and, best of all, free! We had to shoot in the middle of the night so we didn't interfere with anyone else's work schedule.

The director shot alternating closeups of my hands demonstrating the products and wide shots of C. C. and Leanne talking. They used my hands because I had the ability to bring the fabric to life in seconds. Thank goodness I had stopped biting my nails years before because now they were front and center on the television screen. We set up various demonstrations and displays all around the house, so each scene had a different feel.

All the while, I continued negotiations with the two infomercial companies that had been pursuing me. Neither of them knew I was shooting my own infomercial. I did this to keep each competitor at bay and buy myself enough time to get the infomercial shot, edited, and on television. Once the companies got word of what I was doing, I'd have a three- to six-month window of opportunity to maximize my investment before either or both of them hit the air to compete with their own versions of my product. It was inevitable they would knock me off. All I could do was make them believe they had a shot before I lost my own chance. Plus, if for any reason my infomercial wasn't successful, I would still have the opportunity to do it with more experienced professionals and have a second chance for success.

Christmas of 1992 was fast approaching. I thought I needed a familiar face to bring the infomercial together. *The Home Show* hosted by Gary Collins and Sarah Purcell had been a very popular television program at the time. Kitty Bartholomew was the home design expert on the show.

I spent that Christmas with Aunt Paula, Vicky's younger sister. Coincidentally she lived directly across the street from Kitty Bartholomew. At the time I had no idea that she and Kitty were friends. Over dinner Aunt Paula asked what I wanted for Christmas. I said I wanted Kitty Bartholomew to do my infomercial.

Aunt Paula said, "OK. I'll ask her." When she said she would ask Kitty on my behalf it meant the world to me.

Aunt Paula walked over to tell her what I was doing and what a big fan I was and explained how important this favor would be to her. I had an extra $5,000 from an Arts and Crafts

Christmas festival I worked the week before. That was all the money I had left and it was hers if she would agree to it.

My $50,000 budget had slowly climbed into the $65,000 neighborhood. If I failed, it would take another year to earn my savings back. The pressure was on and Aunt Paula had really come through.

Kitty agreed to the money, and she was the perfect choice.

While I was busy editing the infomercial with my team, I had to interview media companies who buy television airtime around the country. I met with three different companies and decided to go with Vikki Hunt from New Day Marketing in Santa Barbara. I had no experience in infomercials and media buying. Vikki took me under her wing and taught me the business. She showed me how to look at and analyze media buys, what the different markets are worth, and how to read the returns on each time slot. At her suggestion we test-marketed the infomercial in five markets. To be honest, five markets were all I could afford.

The test turned out to be a huge success. Vikki said we had a home run on our hands. On March 12, 1993, Kurtain Kraft was on its way to becoming a multimillion-dollar enterprise.

I still had to work trade shows, but now more feverishly than ever. Every dollar I made went to pay for media time because national television time cost a fortune.

Within a few months we went from a small company selling at state fairs and trade shows to a multimillion-dollar corporation. It was the most exciting, adrenaline-pumping roller-coaster ride of my life.

When the infomercial producer who had approached me in Philadelphia discovered I had done an infomercial without him, he actually called to say he appreciated the strategy and congratulated me on its success. The other company I had been in discussions with didn't take the news quite as well. As expected that company knocked off a plastic version of the Kurtain Kraft product line within months.

As the company began to expand, I was still running the day-to-day operation out of my apartment in Marina del Rey. I had no staff, no customer service, and no in-house media manager. I had to hire an entire staff, train them on the product, educate them on the business, and find offices. My brother Johnny came to live with me and help me get set up and organized.

One of the first weeks after Johnny moved in, he and I were driving down Sunset Boulevard on our way to dinner when he turned to me and said, "I have something difficult to tell you." I knew by the tone of his voice that it was going to be a serious conversation. I turned down the radio so I could give him 100 percent of my attention. He proceeded to warn me that this was going to be the most stunning thing he could possibly say. I tried to add some levity by blurting out, "Don't tell me. You're pregnant!" insinuating that he might actually be with child.

He laughed and said, "It's not that bad."

Johnny went on to tell me that he is gay and that I was the first person in the family that he had told. He said he had known for a while but didn't know how to say it. He shared with me that he had a partner, whom he had lived with in Seattle, that he wanted me to meet. I assured him that I had always known and wondered why it had taken him so long to tell me. I didn't care what his orientation was; I loved him and always would. I was eager to meet his partner and suggested he come to Los Angeles. I could tell Johnny was relieved, and frankly so was I. I wanted him to know he could trust me no matter what. And now I knew he did.

Chapter Ten
Failure Is Not an Option

Drive thy business or it will drive thee.   *Benjamin Franklin*

By the end of 1993, nine months after the first airing of the infomercial, Kurtain Kraft had grossed nearly $6 million! I was so elated I took Johnny to Mexico to celebrate all our hard work.

It was my best and worst year in business. It was the best year because I was working so much, and it was the worst year because I was working so hard. My boyfriend, Pat, was in law school. I was working 18-hour days, which were many more hours than I worked when he and I first met the year before. Neither of us had a lot of spare time, so we decided to take a vacation that summer to spend some quality time together. We went to Greece with the understanding that I wasn't supposed to work—a hard promise to keep while running a successful start-up.

Pat watched as everything changed around us. We both came from very humble backgrounds, and suddenly money was plentiful. It was surreal talking about how far we had come and how quickly while sitting on the beautiful black pebble beaches of Santorini. Pat knew what kind of money was being generated and saw how stressed I was. He spent a lot of time on that trip trying to convince me to slow down. He kept telling me to relax because, according to him, I had officially "made it." Pat wanted to finish law school, get married, and start a family. We were young, had lots of money, and could afford a nice house and everything we needed. But by this point, my desire to have children had been extinguished. My brothers and sisters were my kids. I had already raised a family and didn't feel the need to do it again.

I didn't feel as if I had made it yet. I was constantly fighting the desire to do more and be better. Financial security was extremely important to me. When you start making big dollars, it's exciting to be sure, but it's also nerve-racking because the level of responsibility changes with every dollar that comes in. It was an overwhelming sensation for me. Deep down I really didn't know what I was doing. My biggest fear was that everyone else would find out too! I worked as hard maintaining a handle on things as I did on developing new business opportunities. "No" was never an option. Failure wasn't an option. I wasn't about to stop just as I was getting started.

Three days into our trip, I began to get antsy. I was already writing the next infomercial in my mind. I finally gave in to the need to work. I took out a notepad and began writing the script. I also sketched out diagrams for new products to launch after being inspired by a stopover in England on our way to Greece. My mind was exploding with ideas for things I had never seen offered in the United States.

While we vacationed I came up with the idea for a bracket that would allow consumers to create half-moon canopy beds at home. Until I created my product, that look could only be achieved by a professional home installation. My bracket allowed you to do it yourself, using a snap system and premade curtain panels that would be bought through the JCPenney catalog under the name brand of Euro Kraft. These products would be a new brand extension of Kurtain Kraft. It looked exactly the same as the professional bed canopies. This product went on to win several design awards.

After that trip, Pat and I were finished. He was angry with me for not keeping my word to relax and enjoy myself. He was right. I was consumed with working. I had big dreams, goals, and aspirations. I had hoped we would share those experiences, but it wasn't meant to be.

Shortly after we returned from Greece, Vikki sat me down to have a very important conversation. She thought it was time I give up the home shows and fairs. She explained that I was now running a multimillion-dollar corporation that needed my full attention. My focus was too diverted by doing the trade shows and state fairs on weekends. She said she needed me in the office to make big decisions about media, managing the money, and overseeing product fulfillment. Kurtain Kraft had turned into a very big business at the speed of light. Vikki spoke to me like a mentor to a protégé. She could see I was completely exhausted from the grueling schedule. It was in everyone's best interest to cut back on my time commitments to anything other than the core business.

It takes a real friend to tell you the truth, even when you don't want to hear it. If you're smart and thoughtful and pay attention to the big picture, other people's advice will make perfect sense. There are lots of good businesses out there, but they're not always run by good businesspeople. My main goal was to be the best CEO I could be. I was hesitant to let go of the home shows and fairs because it was a business I knew inside and out. It gave me a security blanket because I always knew I could make a living selling in those venues. But, after much thought and deliberation, I gave up the fairs and home shows so I could focus all of my attention on building Kurtain Kraft.

Although I always wanted to remain behind the scenes at my company, the buyers at the television shopping channel QVC were after me to sell Kurtain Kraft products for them on the air. They were pushing me to get in front of the camera. They explained the sales benefit of having a product inventor selling her own products.

I wanted to use Florence Henderson. She was the quintessential mom I always dreamed of having and a perfect choice.

I had already hired Florence Henderson a few months before to host my second infomercial selling Euro Kraft. When we met, she was adamantly against the idea. I wouldn't take no for an answer. I persisted by calling her agent nearly every day, driving him absolutely crazy until Florence said yes. When I got to know her, she was so lovely, supportive, and smart. I thought she was warm and very likable. She was a wonderful host and even agreed to work a trade show, helping me launch the product into retail. My relationship with Florence was so fun and fruitful I thought she would be much more appropriate on-air talent at QVC than me. The executives at QVC disagreed. It wasn't that they didn't love Florence—they did. Still, they insisted that I sell my own products or I couldn't sell them at all. Even though I had no real experience, they agreed to teach me everything there was to know to effectively sell on television. They trained me well. In the end, I loved the rush of being on camera.

Once I began appearing on QVC, I traveled all over the world promoting my products on additional QVC networks in various countries including Germany and England. Doing business with QVC is exciting, but it is also a big financial commitment. You have to be solvent to survive the guaranteed sale policy, meaning you pay to bring the product in, pack it, and ship it, and you don't get paid until after it sells. If your products don't sell, you take them back and absorb all of the costs. There's no negotiating this ironclad policy.

I would rather be a failure doing something that I love than a success doing something that I hate.

George Burns

Starting a business is like climbing Mount Everest. You are either well prepared and have trained for the journey or you will fail. There were months of heavy cash flow and months of being completely strapped while we waited for customers to pay. I always rolled my profits back into the company so it would continue to grow. The infomercial was a cash cow, but my relationship with QVC was turning into a financial drain. The ten-minute segments turned into one-hour shows twice a year that grossed $500,000 per hour. By all standards we should have been making money by the pocketfull. Everything was selling, but the cost to manufacture and the massive inventory along with the extended lengths of time before the products could be sold were suffocating the company. I was too naive and new to the business to really understand what was happening, so I just continued to operate the same as I always had, believing that everything would be fine and eventually the cash flow would even out.

I thought it was a good idea to diversify my marketing and distribution, so I launched Kurtain Kraft into retail about a year after the rollout of the infomercial. It wasn't easy, but I managed to get the first purchase order from Wal-Mart through persistence in calling the buyer, who gave me a big break by placing a large order. I still had a lot to learn. I hadn't created a formal proposal for her; I had only brought the actual product to demonstrate. I asked for her direction in making my pitch because I had no idea what I was doing or what information she needed to know to consider putting my products on her shelves. She was very helpful and made it easy for me to sell to her.

The first big professional presentation I ever made came several months later. I had a meeting at Target. I cold-called Birdie Kissel, the woman who was in charge of buying all the home products. She quickly told me she tried to reach me right after the infomercial aired. She absolutely loved the product. Unfortunately, no one she called would give her a number to reach me. She even called the 800 number from the infomercial, but the person there, thinking she was being protective, declined to give Birdie any information. Worse yet, Birdie told me she had purchased my competitor's product because she wasn't able to find me. I felt sick listening to Birdie describe her failed attempts to reach me.

I tried making light of the situation and continued to apologize profusely for not knowing about her calls. I was embarrassed to ask for a meeting but knew I had one last chance. Thankfully Birdie agreed to see me.

I was a wreck when I walked into her office in Minnesota. I had never made a formal presentation to a big retail chain. I had no idea if my pitch was appropriate or professional.

Birdie could tell I was terribly nervous. I'm sure the presentation was painful for her to watch. I didn't know the first thing about the language or the lingo to effectively communicate my vision. Birdie took the lead and began to show me the ropes. She taught me everything I needed to know to take the company to the next level.

I have found that if you tell people you don't understand something, they'll respect you for being honest. Asking for help doesn't make you weak. On the contrary, it makes you smart.

Chapter Eleven
Humble Pie

Our greatest glory is not in never failing, but in rising each time we fall.

Confucius

By the end of 1995, despite tremendous sales, Kurtain Kraft was struggling. I had minimal margin in the product and I continued to invest all the money that was coming in back into the company.

Although I had been moving a lot of volume through QVC, they hadn't paid on any sales for a long stretch of time. My first purchase order from Wal-Mart was seven figures and they paid in 32 days. I thought everyone would be that timely in their payments! When I tried to collect the nearly seven figures in receivables from QVC however, I was stunned to learn QVC had an exorbitant amount of returns. And although returns are a standard part of the retail business, I wasn't prepared for this volume of returns. I was unaware they existed, as was QVC. They had somehow gotten lost in a warehouse shuffle, and now that they had been found, the money was going to be deducted from my receivables. I had counted on that money. Not receiving this payment was a huge financial strain on the company that forced us to shut down. Despite all the hard work, I had failed and took an enormous blow financially and emotionally.

It was very important to me to make sure I didn't leave anyone financially hanging. I hired a team of lawyers to liquidate all assets, collect all outstanding receivables, and distribute that money as evenly as possible among everyone we owed.

I was devastated. I went from having no money to having lots of money and back to no money again. I found myself eerily alone as I humbly took my fall. I was in such a specialized business that there really was no one else around who knew more about my products and customers than I did.

Swallowing my pride wasn't hard compared to finding the courage to ask people I once had a lucrative relationship with for a leg up when the chips were down. Some of the buyers were very gracious in offering their help so I could figure out what categories to branch into. It made sense for them and was meaningful for me. Having their support really spoke to the fact that business is not just business. Business is always personal. Success is predicated on the quality of your relationships as much as it is on the quality of your products and services. Both can break you or build you.

In an ironic twist of fate, it was QVC that helped build my new company back up by getting me started in the areas of crafts, scrapbooking, and floral design. The former buyer from the home department had moved on to another job. A new regime came in to help relaunch. It was a relief as I had many people depending on the company for their paychecks. I had to get right back up on that horse again. Failure was not an option.

What should happen when you make a mistake is this: You take your knocks, you learn your lessons, and then you move on.
                                        Ronald Reagan

By age 28 I had to start over. My new venture was to become a total lifestyle company. I diversified the product line, creating everything from crafts to gardening products, floral preserving and flower arranging kits, along with a new generation of Kurtain Kraft products. I continued selling on QVC under their company's guidance, direction, and insistence. Consumers essentially dictate the direction of a product line. It is all based on their tastes, buying habits, and desires. I've always been directed by what the consumer wants and QVC helped me hone my skills. My job was to figure out ways to create solution-based products for the busy homemakers' needs and desires. I wanted to design creations that would make them heroes in their home.

Like the old saying goes: "That which does not kill you makes you stronger." This time I had to make sure I didn't make the same mistakes twice. I knew what questions to ask and found ways to protect my investments better.

My mind was like a sponge, especially when it came to educating myself on the ups and downs of business. I spent years developing my relationships with buyers, vendors, CEOs, small business owners, and distributors. My new product lines were extremely diversified. I created several different divisions of the company, allowing us to cater to the widest variety of consumers who were interested in do-it-yourself products.

Target gave me my first big break into gardening. They were focusing on their Garden Place department and needed user-friendly product concepts and kits. They wanted to develop gardening products with the same philosophy that I had been using when creating the home lines. But this time Target wanted my name and likeness on the packaging. I didn't know the first thing about gardening! Gardening was not my forte at the time; I could kill cactus. This admission became the motivation to proceed. If I could do it, anyone could!

Before I knew it I was selling impossible-to-kill gardening products that came in preassembled kits. They included terra-cotta pots, dirt, and seeds—everything you needed to grow healthy plants. The pots were dipped in liquid fertilizer that was released every time the plants were watered, guaranteeing success in the garden. All people had to do was assemble the kit and take all the credit. There were herb, vegetable, and rose gardens along with English and French flower garden combinations—everything a family needed for a fun-filled weekend in the garden together.

My company allowed me to diversify in ways that I hadn't done before. I was presented with many opportunities to branch out into areas I hadn't ever anticipated. I learned so much about all of the home categories and explored new frontiers. It helped me feel even more creative and passionate about what I was doing.

Chapter Twelve
Fighting Through the Shock

Furthermore, tell the people, "This is what the Lord says: See, I am setting before you the way of life and the way of death."
Jeremiah 21:8

My company had taken off, and I was well on my way back up. I finally felt comfortable enough leaving the business to take a much-needed vacation. In August 1997 I decided to take Grandma Lorraine on a cruise to Alaska, a trip she had dreamed about since we traveled to the Holy Land together.

Grandma Lorraine and I met in Vancouver the day we were scheduled to leave port. I immediately noticed she was anxious and uneasy. She absolutely had to get on the boat. She kept telling me we were going to miss the ship and worried that it was going to leave without us. Grandma Lorraine wanted to be among the first passengers on board. I had no idea why she was acting so nervous. I thought she must be excited for our next great adventure. I assured her the boat wouldn't leave without us—pointing out that it wasn't even docked in the harbor from its previous trip. It would be hours before we could board. But Grandma Lorraine insisted we get our bags together and head to the port.

We boarded around 1 p.m. and immediately got settled into our room. We visited the spa, where Grandma got her hair done and I got a massage. We were happy and calm at last. It had been a beautiful sail out of the port. We would be at sea for a full day before reaching our first stop in Alaska.

The ocean shimmered as Grandma and I were seated for dinner in the massive dining room. We chatted away about the vacation to Hawaii we had taken just the year before. We had just ordered our dinner when she turned to me and said, "I am sorry to tell you this, but I have stomach cancer." Her words pierced me like an iceberg through the *Titanic*. But for her it was that matter-of-fact. She said it so abruptly and sharply as if it were the end of a conversation instead of the beginning of one.

She had battled cancer when I was around 10 or 11 years old and already had had part of her stomach and esophagus removed. The doctors were able to get the cancerous tissue out of her body, and, miraculously, she lived a pretty healthy and productive life.

I spent my life listening to Grandma say she would live to be 120 years old because that's what she read in the Bible. This was just fine with me. At 79, she was so energetic and healthy that it was easy to believe her. A strict vegetarian, she could run circles around me. Stomach cancer was a cruel joke, and the fact that she had it again and could possibly die of it was incomprehensible.

In my mind Grandma was invincible and would certainly outlive us all. I couldn't imagine life without her. The very thought sent me into a panic.

My immediate response was that we should get off the ship and seek a second opinion. I wanted to fly her to UCLA

Medical Center, Mayo Clinic, anywhere to see anyone who could aggressively help us fight the disease. She told me her doctor said there was nothing that could be done. I could hear her words, but I couldn't ever accept them. But Grandma Lorraine didn't want any of that.

She began talking about cosmic energy, which was something I had never heard her mention before. She spoke of the gravitational pulls that are caused by the moon that affect the tides and energy on earth, which could affect the outcome of the surgery if she had had it done that very week. It was peculiar to hear her speaking this way because she usually quoted scripture. At the time it sounded like a bunch of babble, an excuse to justify not missing our trip. All I could think about was getting off the ship and rushing her to the hospital.

To appease me, Grandma agreed to get a second opinion the minute we got back if I promised not to let her illness ruin our cruise. I wanted to honor her every request, so I agreed not to make a big deal out of her diagnosis until we were home.

I heard the news of the Princess of Wales' passing while sitting at the captain's table for dinner on the last night of our trip. A man came over to our table and said that Diana had been in a terrible car accident and was dead. I thought the guy was making a terrible joke. Everyone at the table was horrified by his bad taste. I told him he wasn't being funny and that he shouldn't be so flip with his humor. I felt a sharp jolt in my chest and my eyes fluttered in utter disbelief when I realized what he was saying was true. I looked at Grandma, who was sitting between the captain and me. I could see she was just as flustered by the tragic news. I excused myself from the table and rushed back to my cabin to watch CNN. I needed to hear the details for myself.

My reaction to Princess Diana's death was dramatic, if not disproportionate, for a woman I had never met. Like most people, I felt sorry for her circumstances over the years as if she were a personal friend. But of course, she was not. Nonetheless I cried when I heard that she had died. It took me a few minutes to process what happened before I realized my emotional response was being triggered by the unexpected news Grandma shared the day we boarded the ship.

From everyone to whom much is given, much will be required.
Luke 12:48

Despite my promise to have a good time, that final night I couldn't help but stare at my grandmother, thinking this would be our final trip together. I wondered how much time she really had left and if I would have any shot at finding someone who could save her life. The thought of the cancer growing inside of her and attacking her body made me sick.

Although there was an unspeakable tension that lived between us for the entire week on the ship, neither of us said another word about it. The trip lacked the carefree joyfulness we had previously experienced in traveling to places such as Martha's Vineyard and Hawaii. I just wanted to get through the week, get off the boat, and get her home so she could see another doctor. I was willing to take her to see another 200 doctors if that's what it would take.

The truth is, Grandma was tired and didn't have the energy to fight another bout of cancer. Cindy's and my lives were well on their way, so she no longer had to worry about us. Her son Wayne was never going to change. I think she had resigned herself and accepted him for the man he had become. Grandpa Al had passed away years before as had Grandma's brother Harlem and sister-in-law Aunt Betty.

Grandma agreed to follow through with getting a second opinion when we got back from our trip. She came to Los Angeles, where she committed to stay for three extra days before going back to Phoenix, which she now called home. I immediately started making phone calls to every friend I knew who could pull strings to get us into the finest specialists in Los Angeles.

But an hour or two after we got back to my apartment, Grandma came to me and said, "I don't want to get a second opinion. I'm going home."

That's when we got into the only real fight I can remember us ever having. For all of her loveliness, Grandma Lorraine had a stubborn side. I didn't see it often, but there was no budging her when she made up her mind. I began lecturing her on responsibility, telling her she owed it to me to make an effort. I used every tool I had to convince her to go to the doctor. Raising my voice I told her I had already made an appointment and all she had to do was go. I tried to jolt her by saying God would want her to go. I said her great-grandchildren wouldn't get to know her. I tried to guilt-trip her for being selfish. I pulled out all the stops, trying everything I could to get her to change her mind, but she wasn't having it.

She was going to do it her way. She was going home.

I knew I had lost this battle. My only choice was to accompany her back to Phoenix, where she was scheduled to have surgery to try to remove the cancer. Even so the doctors had very little hope for success and told her the cancer was too advanced.

Cindy and I snuck into the recovery room to be with Grandma the moment she came out of the operation. The room was freezing cold. It felt like the morgue she had already been sentenced to—the place I wasn't ready to let her go. I ran to find as many blankets as I could to make sure she was comfortable and warm.

I spent the next seven days at the hospital and getting her house in order to make life easier when she came home. I took her car for a tune-up and new tires, pulled all the weeds from her garden, and organized the carport.

I was running the business by phone from Phoenix and racing to the hospital every chance I had. One morning I arrived a little later than usual. The nurses had to drain water from Grandma Lorraine's lungs because she had developed an infection. No one had called to inform me they were going to do this. I was furious when I walked into the room to discover Grandma propped up with a long needle plunged into her back drawing out the excess fluid.

Grandma Lorraine had a meltdown the minute she saw me, yelling, "Where were you? Look what they did to me and you weren't here!"

I was stunned because in that moment I realized how frightened she had become. Every ounce of me wanted to scoop her up into my arms and carry her out the door, but it was not an option. A few days later Grandma Lorraine was released. I took her home.

Chapter Thirteen
My Worst Fear

When you come to the end of your rope, tie a knot and hang on.
Franklin D. Roosevelt

I was able to get Grandma home and comfortably settled in before I had to leave. She seemed fine and capable so with a heavy heart I flew back to Los Angeles. I had to get back to work. When I returned home I plunged myself into business, trying to numb my emotion and put a salve on my worry. I needed something new to focus on. Food was my next frontier.

Before I left for the cruise with Grandma, Dick Clark and I had partnered to produce a home and garden show for television. He and I had met through our mutual agent and instantly took a liking to one another. We knew there was an opening in the television market for a fresh view on how to conquer the challenges of everything home-related. It was his idea that food be in the forefront of the show. I had always been more than comfortable with baking and felt good about my cooking skills but didn't have as strong a foundation with savory cooking techniques as I wanted.

I had a desire to learn how to make all of the wonderful sauces I had tasted in my travels. I wanted to study at Le Cordon Bleu in Paris or London, but my schedule and responsibilities didn't allow me to be so far away. Le Cordon Bleu had a school in Canada, so I decided to attend classes there in order to expand my knowledge and improve my cooking skills. I wanted to combine quick and easy cooking with great gourmet into a new food concept, something that busy homemakers could use every day.

There are many things I learned when I attended Le Cordon Bleu. One of the most important lessons I took from my experience was experimenting with which combinations of spices worked together to enhance a variety of foods. I also learned more about which are the most interesting side dishes to go along with main course servings to make the most appetizing and flavorful meals. That invaluable experience gave me the knowledge to be creative with my own recipes while writing *Semi-Homemade Cooking*.

I thought there was a huge void in the marketplace for women such as my sisters and my friends who found themselves with too little time to whip up tasty meals made from scratch. Every night in my hotel room, I rewrote the recipes I had learned at Le Cordon Bleu and discovered that I had so many that I could fill an entire book.

The most significant lessons I learned were ways to save time while cooking. Le Cordon Bleu is primarily focused on helping chefs learn to create extravagant meals. I spent hours studying techniques that were ultimately more time-consuming than they were worth for the type of cooking everyday homemakers want and need. For example if you're cooking a veal chop, you have to scrape the tendons off the chop so they don't burn. If you don't the chop looks less appetizing. I spent an hour scraping four chops until they were clean. Who has that type of time and who really cares? Certainly not the overextended, multitasking homemaker I was tending to. Le Cordon Bleu reinforced the importance of presentation—something I had been very thoughtful of while preparing my own special meals at home.

Every day I took what was useful for me and left the rest to the real purists of the culinary world. My primary interest in studying there was to help busy moms find ways to shorten preparation time while achieving the same results with less effort. And though my time at Le Cordon Bleu was a very brief and intense program, I learned so much about cooking during those few weeks. I was in class nine or ten hours every day.

As soon as I got back to Los Angeles, I turned my attention to writing my first cookbook. It would include easy-to-follow recipes using specific brand-name products combined with fresh ingredients. Every recipe had to taste as if it were made from scratch. It had to be great gourmet in minutes.

My book would guarantee home cooks perfect, consistent results every time regardless of their skills in the kitchen. The book would take all of the guesswork out of the process, giving the reader everything needed right down to the name-brand products to use.

To create the recipes, I strolled the aisles of the local grocery store to educate myself on brand names and to learn the ingredient listings of each. I made lists of pantry staple products as well as the ones that are purchased for simple pleasure. I stood frozen in place when I saw the bags of Toll House semisweet chocolate chips. Everyone keeps an emergency bag of chocolate chips on hand. Something clicked in my head. Semisweet . . . Semi-Homemade. I knew the name of my book and this particular approach to cooking from here on in would be known as Semi-Homemade.

Further the Semi-Homemade approach would perfectly represent the layout of every grocery store and the shopping habits of its guests. Seventy percent of every store is in lined aisles with thirty percent of the store making the perimeter. With Semi-Homemade this would translate to seventy percent of each recipe being either boxed, canned, jarred, or frozen with thirty percent fresh ingredients including meat, baked goods, and produce.

I wondered if the name Semi-Homemade was meaningful, memorable, and clear enough to explain the concept so I shared this idea with Dick Clark, and he loved it. He encouraged me to develop it as quickly as possible, which I did. I wrote a book proposal, got a literary agent, and presented the idea to every publisher in New York who would take a meeting. I was rejected by every publisher. My only hope of launching Semi-Homemade was to publish the book myself. I believed this would fill the void in the market and help the overextended homemaker. I was willing to take that financial risk myself.

I set out to find a designer and a food photographer, set up a studio, source a printer, and develop a budget for the book. Once again I'd be risking savings, but I was passionate about Semi-Homemade. The bright side to self-publishing was that I would have complete creative freedom, producing Semi-Homemade exactly the way I envisioned it.

I produced the book and printed 50,000 copies. I primarily sold *Semi-Homemade Cooking* through television shopping channels and small ma-and-pa booksellers. Semi-Homemade was an instant hit. My home hero loved it. The "home heroes" to me are the real heroes. They are the homemakers who fight every day to make ends meet while taking care of children, family, home-keeping, and finances. They do this without the support of nannies or housekeepers, and few have time or money left over for extras. But they still find a way to make everything special. They know their homes and meals are the places where memories are fostered and quality time is never inconsequential. They are the Grandma Lorraines of the world. To me they are the true unsung heroes.

Grandma will always be my original home hero, but in early February of 1998, Cindy called to say Grandma Lorraine didn't look well. She was only 80 years old but she was weak and deteriorating and had fallen several times. Cindy told me to come back to Phoenix right away.

When I arrived it quickly became clear to me that Grandma could no longer live on her own. There was no way we were putting her into a home. Grandma and I talked about the options and decided that a live-in nurse would be a great solution for her. The trick? Finding someone she trusted and liked. We interviewed dozens of nurses until we found two who would each spend 12 hours a day in her home. I knew I couldn't be with her full-time because of my business so I was thrilled when she found two nurses she wanted. For the most part they were there to be more like companions than medical assistants. It gave us great peace of mind to know they were there playing cards and keeping Grandma company while watching over her well-being.

I spent the next week with her too. I sat with Grandma for days, doing my best to keep her comfortable. Her feet were constantly ice cold and swollen. She was retaining fluid around her ankles, and the massive amounts of water pills she was taking weren't helping. I bought her a foot spa and filled it with hot water, hoping to reduce the inflammation and pain. I let her sit for a bit before I propped her foot up on my knee. I applied gentle pressure and massaged her from her calves down to her ankles and into her toes, releasing as much pressure as I could by dissipating the fluid. I wrapped her feet in towels and placed her in bed.

I climbed into bed with her that night. We talked about everything, just like we did when I was a little girl. We talked about her family and friends and went through a lifetime of dreams and desires. It was one of the most intimate conversations we ever had.

On Thursday evening, I left Arizona feeling assured that she would be fine for a long while to come. My business needed my attention. Kimmy and I had an on-air commitment at QVC that weekend. I promised Grandma I'd be back as soon as I was finished, hugging and kissing her goodbye.

On my way back from that trip, I had a change of planes in Chicago. It was a Sunday night. When I checked my voice mail, I had received a frantic message from Carol, one of Grandma's friends, to call as soon as I could. The battery on my cellular phone died just as I received that message so I had to find a phone booth. When I called Grandma, Carol answered the phone and said I needed to come right away. The tone in her voice was serious and instantly communicated that Grandma was in grave condition.

There were only two flights leaving Chicago that I could possibly make that night. One went direct to Phoenix and the other, which I was already booked on, went to Los Angeles. I ran to the Phoenix gate first, hoping they would understand my dire situation but I was too late. The flight was full, and the gate was closed. I had an emotional breakdown, trying to explain everything to the gate attendant. I was sobbing, barely able to communicate. I pleaded with her to stop the plane. I offered her money, telling her I would pay her anything if she would get me on that flight. I was desperate. I had to get to Phoenix. But there was nothing she could do. The plane had already pulled away from the gate. I was forced to take the last plane to Los Angeles that night.

When I boarded the plane, I could feel the other passengers staring at me as I took my seat. I was crying and emotional. I used the phone on the plane to call Cindy and tell her to immediately get to Grandma's house. I cried the entire first half of the flight. I tried to close my eyes and still myself, but I could not. I stared out the window at the bright, full moon suspended in the blue-black sky at 39,000 feet. I visualized all of Grandma's family and friends in my mind, the collection of greeters that would gather to welcome her into heaven. Her father, her grandmother, and the other friends I knew who had passed. I thought of all the familiar faces that I prayed would be there for her in my absence. It seemed I recognized everyone, even those people I had only seen in pictures. I remembered them all in an instant.

Grandma Lorraine died while I was in flight. A friend told me the news when I got off the plane. I was inconsolable at the airport, nearly hysterical.

I later discovered that the time of Grandma Lorraine's passing was nearly the same moment I had envisioned the gathering of her loved ones welcoming her into heaven.

That night I felt a pain that I had never before experienced. I didn't sleep and I couldn't eat. I called my best girlfriend, Colleen, and my Aunt Peggy. They both knew what happened the second they heard the emptiness that had filled my heart and clearly consumed my voice. To me the pain felt bottomless, as though it would never end. Colleen talked to me about my grandmother until 3:30 in the morning. She told me to take a hot shower before going back to the airport.

Many times in my life I have felt as if it wasn't me going through all of the stunning events that had taken place. The one thing I had never felt until now was pure emptiness and blinding sadness. This was a loss that would never heal.

I stood in the shower and sobbed. I put my hand against the wall to hold myself up. Grandma Lorraine was my North Star, always there to guide me home. I was going to be lost without her.

Throughout my life, Grandma provided me with a platform of options and gifts wrapped in unconditional love and adorned with a bow of complete support. She was always available, willing to sacrifice her own needs to ensure my success and providing the tools that would allow me to survive. She was the greatest gift of my entire life.

I could not go to sleep. It was already 4:30 in the morning, so I would soon be leaving for the airport anyway. I was drained and fatigued, emotionally fragile and physically worn down. In the last six hours, my life had completely changed.

Aunt Peggy met me at LAX airport and we flew to Phoenix together on the first flight out. We rushed to Grandma's house where Cindy was waiting to meet us. She was lucky enough to have arrived as Grandma was taking her last breaths. She was the one there to hold her throughout the transition from life to death. When I walked into the house, Cindy told me that Carol, Grandma's best friend from church, had filled her room with candles as she read to Grandma from the scriptures.

I wanted to climb into bed with Grandma Lorraine and hold her for hours. Of course, I didn't. I just looked at her and cried. There was no life in her body, no wrinkles in her face. She looked different to me, and I was afraid of her at first. I was frightened by death; it was evil, and I hated it. I have never said that out loud. I have only written that for the first time now. I was ashamed that I was afraid of my grandmother's body in death. But I loved her dearly and didn't want to say goodbye.

Looking back, there aren't many moments in my life I would change, but not being there when Grandma passed away is certainly one of them. I have found peace in knowing all my experiences have made me who I am today. If I had had a different life, different experiences, or events which were timed differently I'd be a different person. This is the path God chose for me, and I believe that a person's mission in life is to follow his or her path to the best of their ability. One of our greatest challenges in life is how we deal with the situations we've been presented.

Grandma Lorraine taught me to live each and every day in the moment. To take the time to tell loved ones you care. To say "I love you" every day to your kids, spouse, or family. Don't go to bed angry. To be loving and kind. To always take the high road. I learned that if you strive to live each day as if it were your last, you will find more peace, love, joy, and meaning in your life. Grandma taught me to make a difference whenever I could and how important it was to make my life matter. I'm not sure she ever knew she was teaching me these lessons. I learned by watching her.

And surely I am with you always, to the very end of the age.
Matthew 28:20

I didn't dream about Grandma Lorraine for at least a year after she died. I couldn't understand why she wasn't coming to me in my dreams. And then one night there she was. I was so angry with her in that dream, and I asked her where she had been. Why didn't she come to me sooner? I wanted to know how I could talk to her, see her, and feel her presence. Even in my dream, I was aware enough of her absence in my conscious life to scold her like a child. When I awoke I was shocked that I had had the presence of mind to let her know how angry I was.

In my dream she did her best to explain that she'd been busy. She said, "There's so much going on up here in heaven, honey, you can't imagine!" She told me how wonderful it is and if I thought I was having fun here, wait until I get up there! She looked beautiful, just as she did when she was a young woman. She loved showing me how pretty she was, and I was so happy for her joy.

I find great peace in knowing that Grandma is happy. In a way, seeing her in my dreams, even rarely, allows me to stay connected, something I wanted and almost expected after she died. Though she doesn't come to me often when I dream, I am certain she watches over me like my own guardian angel in heaven.

Chapter Fourteen
A Final Goodbye

The turning point in the process of growing up is when you discover the core of strength within you that survives all hurt.

Max Lerner,
The Unfinished Country

I flew back to Los Angeles a couple of days after Grandma passed away. I was emotion in motion. The funeral was scheduled a week after she died. I would return to Phoenix a few days before. When I arrived at the airport, the airline insisted I didn't have a seat. I like to think I am a very organized person. It would have been very unusual for me to botch making a plane reservation, especially for my grandmother's funeral. Despite my certainty, they still refused to let me on the flight. I burst into tears on the spot.

As I begged the agent behind the counter to find a seat for me, my cell phone rang. I thought it was Cindy calling to find out when I would arrive, but the phone number on my caller ID came up as private. When I answered there was a man's voice on the other end. It was Bruce Karatz, the CEO of Kaufman and Broad Homes, a company I was now working with as a consultant. It was the first time he ever called me. He explained that his head of marketing had resigned and he wanted to discuss his company's future marketing plans.

I tried to pull myself together so Bruce wouldn't know I was falling apart, but I couldn't stop sobbing. His call was the ultimate in bad timing! Bruce could tell that something was terribly wrong. When I explained that my grandmother had passed away, he was wonderfully sympathetic and surprisingly comforting. From then on he periodically checked back to see how life was going.

Finally the airline found a seat for me on the flight to Phoenix. I spent the days leading up to the funeral going through Grandma Lorraine's things. I read all the old love letters from Grandpa Al, letters from her brother, every card and letter I gave her, and any other correspondence she had tucked away like a rare time capsule. It was at this time I discovered the letters from Vicky telling Grandma Lorraine she could see Cindy and me if she sent money every month. My heart sank when I made this discovery. In my eyes, my mother had all but blackmailed my grandmother for visitation. Money had to be paid for access to the grandchildren this woman had loved and nurtured in Vicky's absence. I was shocked and disgusted and felt a rage I had never experienced before.

After hours of reading and research, I had finally compiled a complete overview of Grandma's amazing and inspirational life. It was hugely important for me to have the right words to share on the day of her funeral.

Grandma's funeral was standing room only at her church in Mesa, Arizona. Cindy and I organized the music, flowers, and the gathering afterward. Before she passed I asked Grandma Lorraine to record her favorite Bible verses, which we played during the service. I loved hearing her voice one final time. Cindy and I placed photos of Grandma on the pew and proceeded with a moving and emotional celebration of her life. The overall feeling was much more of a party than a funeral. In a way I felt as if I were planning her 90th birthday party! She would have loved it.

I had placed my speech on the podium ahead of time so that when it was time to speak, I wouldn't have to carry the pages with me. Cindy stood at my side, silent, but full of strength as I began. By the second sentence I could feel that familiar sensation of my throat closing, my chest tightening, and my nose swelling as I desperately tried to hold back my tears. My head was dizzy with emotion. I couldn't go on. I turned to walk back to my seat, unable to finish the beautiful eulogy I had worked so hard to write.

Cindy snapped up my speech and began delivering it with sheer perfection. When I realized she was reading my words I got up and grabbed the pages right out of her hands and took over. We nudged each other out of the way, practically bantering back and forth as we tried to share the words on the page through our tears. It was a wonderful release of the emotional energy we had built up and a true demonstration of how much we both loved Grandma Lorraine and each other. We were the only two people in the church who had the pleasure of Grandma our entire lives. By the time we finished, everyone else knew how much we loved her, how extraordinary her life had been, and the impact she had made.

After the funeral I spent the next night at Cindy's. My niece Danielle was still little and my nephew Austen was just a baby. We decided to barbecue around the pool that night. I went into the kitchen to start preparing dinner while Cindy put Austen to bed. Carrying a large tray full of food outside to be grilled, I headed out to the pool. I opened the gate and placed the platter next to the grill. I lifted the lid of the barbecue, when out of the corner of my eye I noticed something moving at the far end of the pool area. I wasn't aware that Danielle had followed me. She was standing at the edge of the pool reaching for a ball that was in the water. What happened next was a nightmare that came to life. I watched my niece fall into the water and disappear. I dropped the plate I was holding and ran as fast as I could to the other end of the pool. As I looked into the water, I could see her eyes wide open and her body stiff and rigid as she looked up at me. I jumped into the water to pull her out and wrapped my arms around her. I could feel her clenched tightly to me. As we surfaced she let out a loud cry. She cried all the way into the house. We were both shaking and scared. I took her right into a hot shower and held her until we both calmed down.

I was furious with myself for not keeping an eye on Danielle. All of those intense protective feelings I had for my siblings from so many years ago flooded through my head and heart in that instant. I could see Kimmy standing on the slippery rocks by the bank of the river, Johnny up on the highway trying to trip a car with a rake, and Richie in the cornfield building a bonfire, trying to light his matches. It was amazing to me that I had carried that fear and that it all came back so quickly with the scare from my niece. In a single moment all the love

I had for my brothers, sisters, and Grandma transferred into my nieces and nephews. Although I had been in the room when Kimmy gave birth to my first nephew, Scottie, and I instantly loved him, I hadn't felt the extreme sense of responsibility I would have for the kids until this near tragedy with Danielle. The thought of losing any of them was too much to bear.

Wayne found his way to Phoenix to collect his expected inheritance though he did not attend Grandma's funeral. As far as I could tell, he thought he had hit a home run the day Grandma Lorraine died. She had a couple of hundred thousand dollars in the bank and owned her home outright. As the executor of the estate, I had the job of making sure her final wishes were carried out. I helped Grandma Lorraine write her Last Will and Testament, so I knew where all the money was directed. Half of her estate was earmarked for Wayne, and the remaining half was being distributed among her other heirs. I had no interest in Grandma's money. What was important to me were her personal belongings, heirlooms, photos, and family memorabilia which is what I received.

Wayne was relentless until he received his half of the estate. I was afraid he might do something stupid like try to ransack the house. Instead he wanted to live in it. I tried to show compassion every time I took one of Wayne's angry calls because he was a man who had just lost his mother. I wanted to believe his actions were from remorse and grief. Even so, I knew I had to rid myself of Wayne and his threatening, aggressive demands once and for all.

One of the belongings I kept after Grandma passed away was an old pair of her favorite shoes. She wore them practically every day. To me they are a daily reminder that until you've walked in someone else's shoes, it would be impossible to know the challenges they faced, the adversity they've overcome, and what their life has been like. I have always been inspired by the popular poem "Footprints in the Sand," because it was my Grandma's favorite poem and it reminds us that we are never alone and that no matter who you are or where you're from, sometimes everyone needs a helping hand.

Various versions of this poem exist and many different writers have taken credit for writing it, but their story is the same. In simple verses it recounts a vivid dream in which the poet is walking along a beach with the Lord. And as they walk, scenes from the poet's life appear vividly, including "footprints in the sand." The poet is troubled by the vision because only one set of footprints was apparent during periods of hardship or anguish, upset that the Lord must have been absent at those times. The Lord offers a comforting correction: "When you have seen only one set of footprints, my child, is when I carried you."

Grandma Lorraine would understand and appreciate the importance of those footprints, and I am fortunate to have been "carried" on more than one occasion by her strength and spirit as she walked through life.

So I treasure her shoes as a reflection of Grandma, who lived her entire life offering kindness, love, and understanding to every person she met. I keep her shoes in my closet to remind me of how hard Grandma worked and of all the sacrifices she made for my sister and me.

It was two weeks before Grandma was laid to rest. Although the funeral was held in Arizona, her wish was to be buried next to her mother in Santa Monica. The mortuary kept calling to say I had to set a burial date, but the thought of my final farewell made it impossible for me to schedule that time. I felt paralyzed for those two weeks. Every time they called it became a reminder of the inevitable nightmare from which there would be no waking once their request was granted.

I had never dealt with death before. I didn't know how to handle the emotional drain of losing Grandma and the non-stop aching in my heart. Burying someone you love is a very intense thing. Although there was nothing I could have done to change the outcome, it still felt as if I were responsible for sealing my grandmother's fate.

She must have known how I would feel as she had already planned everything out. She chose the mortuary and her final resting place. She was the type of woman who never wanted to bother anyone with details and would have done it all herself if she could.

The day I dreaded more than any other finally arrived. Cindy and I spent hours picking out the clothes that Grandma Lorraine would be buried in. We chose the beautiful pink dress and matching bonnet that she wore to Cindy's wedding. We placed her favorite pictures of my sister and me inside her old tattered Bible. I was very torn about wanting to keep the Bible for myself because it was her most valued possession. I knew Grandma believed in the resurrection, so she would want her Bible with her for the rest of eternity. I gently placed it in her hands, which were draped across her chest, so it would be secure forever.

I thought I had put it in the perfect place, but my sister looked at me as if I were nuts. She has a certain expression that makes me feel as if I am the dumbest blond on the planet. Cindy insisted we put the Bible under the belt of Grandma's dress for fear it might fall off her body during an earthquake! I know this might sound amazing, and even as I write it, it stuns me as well that we were negotiating the minutest details where everything was hyperimportant and ultrasensitive.

We held a second, smaller service at the church in Santa Monica where Grandma had run the community service program for 25 years. It was only after I walked through the doors that I realized it was the very church where Cindy and I had committed our Wheat Thins crime so many years ago. I invited friends whom Grandma had known some 40 years or more, many of whom I vaguely remembered from my childhood. I didn't want a large gathering at the cemetery, so I limited the attendance at the service.

At the cemetery just a few gathered and said a short prayer together, after which we paused for a moment of silence. I closed my eyes, took a deep breath, and exhaled. I opened my eyes just as Grandma Lorraine's casket hit the dirt and I heard a loud thump. I swear I saw the lid shift a few inches. All I could think was that bugs and dirt were getting inside the coffin. I kept visualizing myself jumping into the grave to secure the lid back in place. There wasn't a scoop of dirt on the casket yet and I was worried that Grandma was getting dirty. My head was spinning from what I knew were irrational thoughts. I finally convinced myself that everything was fine. And once I did, I could breathe again.

I needed a moment to collect my thoughts. A cemetery worker asked if they could start shoveling in the dirt. I wasn't ready for that. I told them to just leave the shovels. I'd take care of it.

I turned, looked at Cindy, and said in a whisper, "Grab a shovel." I began shoveling dirt onto her casket. All I could think of was that no one was going to bury Grandma but us. She was ours. I forced myself not to break down but I had a silent stream of tears running down my cheeks. No one said a word. I looked up at Cindy and wondered why she wasn't helping. She blankly stared back at me, consumed in her own grief, unsure of why I was glaring at her. And then it hit her. She jumped forward, grabbed a shovel, and began placing her scoops of dirt on top of mine. We shoveled the entire pile of dirt back into the hole. Burying Grandma ourselves felt like a final gift to her. To the woman who had loved us so selflessly and to the woman who made us who we were.

The last thing that needed to be taken care of was Grandma Lorraine's headstone. I had ordered the stone before the funeral, expecting to have it in place the week after her burial. It took a little longer than planned to have it engraved just the way I wanted and it wasn't ready on time. Before I knew it, a month had passed. Life was moving on and I was filling every day as full as I could. I needed to stay busy to block out the sadness, but in the back of my mind I knew that Grandma would have been hurt if she knew I had not returned to the cemetery to oversee this final detail; and I needed to go back for me too.

When I finally went, I had not called or made an appointment. I assumed her headstone would be in place and I walked around the cemetery in a daze, searching for her grave. I remembered it being near a tree. I grew frantic trying to find her. Suddenly I couldn't remember the sound of her voice. I closed my eyes and tried to hear her.

It had only been a few weeks.

How could I have forgotten?

I clutched the bouquet of flowers I brought so tightly, my knuckles turned white. I was panicking.

Where is she?

Where did I leave her?

How could I forget?

I should have come sooner. I was racked with guilt for not being there to place her headstone myself. My heart was pounding through my chest and my eyes were stinging with fresh tears.

Off in the distance, I saw a group of people gathered around talking. As I approached I could see they were cemetery workers. My voice was shaky as I asked them for help finding my grandmother's grave. I gave them her name with the hope they could show me the way. They looked shocked. That's when I noticed they were all gathered around a grave placing a headstone. I could hardly believe my eyes when I read her name. The stone must have taken longer than I imagined. It wasn't planned, but I was miraculously standing at her grave the moment her stone was being placed. I knelt down to check the spelling just to make sure it was correct.

I had to accept that Grandma Lorraine was gone, but to this day I haven't gone back to the cemetery in Santa Monica. It's not the way I want to remember Grandma, and the thought of going there is still overwhelming.

After the burial I suggested to my brothers and sisters that we all get together and spend some quality time. The thought of losing any of them was too much to bear after Grandma died. I desperately needed to spend time with my family to feel safe and connected while I mourned. Even though Kimmy, Johnny, and I worked together, it wasn't necessarily time spent where we could just enjoy one another's company and have fun. And up to this point, our family holidays were primarily spent running around, getting things done instead of focusing on relaxed bonding time. Because all of us worked, it was impossible to get everyone together at the same time. I suggested we all meet at Whistler Mountain in Canada for a week during my nieces' and nephews' spring break. Everyone agreed it was a great idea. I wanted to spend a week with my family during which there would be no worries—just having fun and being together.

This is your time here to do what you will do . . . your life is now.   *John Mellencamp*

We booked a string of connecting rooms in a local lodge where the kids could run freely from room to room. During the day the kids went to snowboarding school while the rest of us went off to ski. Every night held something new and exciting, from sleigh rides to a candlelit cabin where we had a wonderful dinner to snowmobiling in the moonlight down the backside of the mountain. By far our favorite time was spent around the heated pool, where the kids got to swim and we were able to put our feet up in front of the outdoor fire pit. That week brought us closer together as a family than we had ever been before. It helped us appreciate how important we were to one another as well as our responsibility and commitment to ensuring that we would all be there for one another's children, filling in any void or need that they might have. We all wanted to be sure that none of our children would ever experience the things we had while growing up.

Chapter Fifteen
Overwhelmed by Emptiness

Life is 10 percent what happens to me and 90 percent how I react to it.   *Lou Holtz, famous football coach*

For nearly a year after the vacation in Whistler, I militantly and blindly threw myself back into work. On the surface everything looked fine, but deep down all of my joy had been snuffed out by loss and loneliness. My grandma was gone.

I was consulting with Kaufman and Broad and working on the development of an infomercial to sell new homes. Because I was the only member of the team who had successfully produced an infomercial, my experience gave me a lot of clout in determining the best way to get an effective infomercial on the air. The concept was simple. The consumers could pick and purchase a lot and build the home of their dreams using one of the country's largest builders. The owner could select every detail of the home from the finishings, the faucets, hardware, garage doors, flooring, and appliances to colors and even siding. Every expense would be rolled into the mortgage loan, minimizing out-of-pocket costs while allowing the new homeowners to completely personalize every inch of their living space.

When Kaufman and Broad's director of marketing left, Bruce began to rely more heavily on me to shepherd the infomercial project from start to finish. We had a great working relationship. After the infomercial was complete, an unexpected friendship began to develop between Bruce and me, and we quietly started dating.

I was starting to lose interest in my own business. After running like the Energizer Bunny for so many years, I needed a break. I was exhausted. But all of my passion for business disappeared when I received a call from my product manufacturer explaining why his most recent shipment was late. The truck transporting my inventory had missed a narrow corner and careened off the mountainside killing both the driver and the warehouse manager. I felt horribly guilty that my business had caused other people to feel the same loss that I had when Grandma passed away. I no longer wanted to climb on pallets or worry about trucking companies, nor did I want to feel this guilt.

I was going through the motions of work, but my heart was no longer in it. I couldn't ever remember not wanting to work. The feeling of total burnout scared me. You hear about people throwing in the towel, quitting, and walking away from lucrative jobs all the time. I never ever thought that person would someday be me. I was once too motivated and committed to success to let a bout of depression hold me back. But even that fire was gone.

By 1999 I could no longer live with the constant stress in my life. I simply couldn't take it anymore, so I took a hiatus and decided to travel. I needed time to reassess my situation. I wanted to be sure I was ready to give everything up. Time and space away from the daily grind would provide me with the clarity I needed to make a decision.

My first stop was Paris, where Kimmy flew to meet me. We planned to spend a few weeks touring Europe in between a few last obligations for work. My relationship with Bruce had transitioned into something more romantic. He was an older, suave, and sophisticated gentleman who was also successful and worldly and possessed a tremendous energy. Everything Bruce did he did with style and elegance. He enjoyed good food and fine wine. He had been everywhere I had, and every place I wanted to go.

Bruce happened to be working in Paris when Kim and I were there to attend the French Open. He took us to dinner on the patio at Le Bristol Hotel. It was the most beautiful garden restaurant I had ever seen. It was a courtyard garden where the walls had been adorned with white lattice crawling with white roses and wispy ivy vine. The night was surreal and a great escape from my life back home. It was the first time in many years I felt calm and carefree. I no longer felt the need to worry about business.

I was supposed to be in Germany at QVC Monday morning. Bruce asked if I had any interest in seeing Saint-Tropez for the weekend. I had been there before and loved Saint-Tropez. I was delighted to accept Bruce's invitation to go back. I was looking forward to spending some time alone with him.

We spent three days buzzing around on mopeds and soaking up the exotic sun at the beautiful beach clubs. My favorite was Club 55, which was filled with the most interesting people walking about—some on their way to lie topless on the beach and others to lounge comfortably on the overstuffed white couches and chairs that were set under a large canvas-covered veranda.

Twilight in Saint-Tropez was spent strolling around the cobblestone port, wandering in and out of the shops, and eating Grand Marnier cherry crepes made by the vendors who lived in the village. Eating those crepes seemed so special to me. They were easy to make and yet tasted wonderful. I walked away wondering what quick technique my Grandma would have used to make these simple yet delicious indulgences at home.

In the evenings Bruce took me to Villa Romana for dinner. Everything was fabulous, from the grand piano that had been converted into a dining room table to the bar that was lit from end to end with live fire. Huge vases filled with large goldfish were set on top of gilded baroque tables throughout the restaurant. Every day in Saint-Tropez was a dream. I can still smell the jasmine that filled the air.

It was hard to leave Bruce at the end of the weekend because we had such a spectacular trip. He made me feel safe and secure every bit as much as he made me feel smart and beautiful. We flew back to Paris together before Bruce left on his private jet for California and I boarded my flight to Germany.

I stood in Charles de Gaulle with tears in my eyes. I didn't want the weekend to end. In a way I felt as if Bruce were a gift from Grandma Lorraine after she died. He came into my life the week she passed. He was established and stable, everything Grandma would have wanted for me and everything I needed.

While I was in Saint-Tropez, my sister flew to Germany to get organized so we could sell through whatever product was left in our storage facility at QVC. It was the last place on earth I wanted to be.

I spent the next while traveling as planned. I went to Greece, Costa Rica, and England. It allowed me the time and space I needed to make one of the most difficult and yet easiest decisions of my professional life. I saw so many new things and experienced lifestyles different from those in the United States. Living in South America is a totally different experience from living in Italy. The formal, elegant European lifestyle is hugely unlike the fun-natured ease of life south of the border. I absorbed as much as I could about the various cultures, traditions, foods, and products native to every country I visited.

That time away completely changed how I felt about what I wanted to do with my life. I realized that you didn't have to be rich or famous to enjoy the pleasures of faraway places in your home. It taught me the same thing Grandma passed on to me growing up—a home is special because of traditions. I wanted to concentrate on ways to improve people's quality of life instead of focusing on creating product lines and developing departments for buyers.

After touring abroad, I decided to come home and figure out how to put a plan into action for the rest of my life. The first thing I did was close down my company.

Chapter Sixteen
Blissful Beginnings

Many persons have the wrong idea about what constitutes true happiness. It is not attained through self-gratification, but through fidelity to a worthy purpose.   *Helen Keller*

For the next two years, my life was a fairy tale full of wonder and enchantment. Everything I had read in my Danielle Steel novels came to life with Bruce, and I felt like a real-life Cinderella. We spent nearly all of our time traveling. We had moved in together and I was free from all of my business obligations. My only job was to have fun and be ready to go on a moment's notice. And go is exactly what we did. It was a nonstop schedule that included frequent trips to Paris and the South of France. Le Bristol Hotel became my second home. The famous Rue du Faubourg in Saint-Honoré became a playground for shopping couture and lunching with the ladies every day from 1 to 3 p.m. We'd gather at a restaurant called L'Avenue on Avenue Montaigne, which all of the chicest of chic Parisians frequented.

The nights in Paris were the most romantic, especially dinners at the ultratrendy Hôtel Costes, located off of the Place de la Concorde. The open-air patio was magical with beautiful women and elegant men. Then it was off to go dancing at The Ritz. Later we would relax with a nightcap under the stars at Plaza Athenee.

Bruce spoke fluent French and had been named a chevalier, the grandest French honor. It was similar to a knighthood and allowed us entré everywhere we went as if we were royalty. We visited castles in the country and enjoyed hours of carefree lunches, sharing stories of our lives and how we built our businesses. Bruce and I became inseparable. We had also quickly settled into our own annual routine.

May was always spent in Paris, timed perfectly to the French Open tennis tournament. This was a special occasion because we celebrated the anniversary of the first time we'd met in Paris. I loved watching the international tennis matches and felt privileged to be sitting in the special box seats.

June was spent in Saint-Tropez, which was the most cherished place to us as this was where we spent our first weekend away together. We went to our favorite beach club every day, lounging in the sun and drinking the local French rosé wine. From time to time we would run into friends from all over the world. There was always something new and exciting to be explored and enjoyed.

Nights were spent in the port that sits in front of the ancient beach village, party-hopping from yacht to yacht, each more decadent than the last. Nearly every night we ended up in the same place, the nightclub at the Hotel Byblos, dancing until the wee hours of the morning, gazing at all of the celebrities who dotted the room like the endless stars in the French Riviera sky.

Whenever I was out and about in Saint-Tropez, I was always searching for the most famous resident of the village—the ultimate blond, Brigitte Bardot. She lives there year-round and still carries the same mystique as in her original days in film. In the more than ten years I have visited Saint-Tropez, I never have seen her.

July was spent in Capri, an Italian island off the coast of Naples. We'd fly over by helicopter, landing on an island that looked as if time hadn't touched it since the Roman era. To me it was like Fantasy Island. I half expected to see the ever-elegant Ricardo Montalban from the famous television show greeting us when we landed.

There are no cars in Capri by the city center, only small carts transporting luggage. The villagers always chanted, "Luggage in, luggage out." Endless shops lined the worn stone streets, and the hotels seemed to be built right into the cliff sides, each boasting it had the most magnificent view of the rock formations scattered in the ocean around the island. Capri is one of the most naturally beautiful architectural places imaginable.

The morning air was clean and crisp as we began each day with a long walk through the pass leading to the ancient Roman ruins and finished with cappuccino and croissants at a local cafe. Days were spent boating, swimming, and sunning, going from island to island. In 30 minutes we could be in Positano for lunch or Ravello for dinner. Nights in Capri were starry and still. The moon that hung large and low on the water illuminated the island and cast a shimmer that only exists in this magical place.

August was spent back home in Los Angeles, where life was just as fun and full. On Saturdays and Sundays Bruce and I would go golfing and lunching at the country club. Sharon Davis, the former first lady of California, and I had become very friendly. She took me to get my first set of golf clubs. We occasionally golfed together, and I am certain my game was painful for her to watch. She insisted Henry-Griffitts were the most special and helpful clubs and would significantly improve my game. They were custom-made and fit to perfection. I worked hard on my swing every chance I could so I wouldn't embarrass myself or slow up my golfing partners.

During the week my life was full of errands and social planning. There were always dinners out and parties to attend as well as the occasional opening and charitable fundraiser.

The Los Angeles Lakers games were the biggest scene. We had season tickets next to Burt Sugarman and Mary Hart, who were as enthusiastic for our hometown team as we were. Burt and Mary quickly became our good friends, and we looked forward to aggressively cheering on our Lakers and booing their opponents together. Mary and I developed a nice friendship over the next few years. She advised me like an older sister on everything I asked, giving me pointers on Hollywood etiquette and strongly suggesting I keep my focus on my talents and career.

Mary is a self-made, independent woman who is as smart as she is sweet. When she wasn't working she spent her time with her family or serving as a member of the board of directors at Childrens Hospital. Mary constantly hosted retreats and organized fundraising events.

She and I would catch up at lunches after she finished shooting her television show, *Entertainment Tonight*. Whenever she called me it was always such a pleasure to hear her voice. "Sandra Lee? It's Mary Hart!" she sang, always up, cheerful, and warm.

Another couple with whom Bruce and I became very friendly were Ray and Ghada Irani. Ray sat on Bruce's board of directors in the United States and France, which often allowed Ghada and me to spend time together. We chatted like schoolgirls, sharing all of our secrets and dreams. Ghada has always been inclusive and available, even though she is married to one of the most powerful men in the world. From the moment we met, Ghada always made me feel important and welcome. Many of the wives weren't especially nice. I felt as if they thought I was young, naive, and unrefined. I felt their definition of "unrefined" meant stuck up and aloof—two words that I would never want to describe me. And I certainly never wanted to share their air of arrogance.

Find a need and fill it.   *Henry J. Kaiser, Industrialist*

One day Ghada and I were lunching at Wolfgang Puck's restaurant, Spago, in Beverly Hills. She was talking about creating a board of directors for a new chapter of UNICEF she was starting in Los Angeles. She already had the commitment of Arda Yemenidjian, whose husband was one of the big movie studio executives. Ghada was wondering if I might join their dynamic duo. We would be the Three Musketeers for UNICEF. She shared with me all of the good works and lifesaving initiatives we would be focusing on. It was a new kind of work, and saving children was certainly much more important than anything I had done before.

I was thrilled with the invitation and immediately said yes. Ghada, Arda, and I spent the next year planning our first fundraising event and securing corporate and private donations. We worked diligently to get our new chapter off the ground.

Our event was called the First Annual Los Angeles Snow Flake Ball. It was held at the Beverly Hilton hotel, where the Golden Globe Awards take place. It was a winter wonderland theme, with everything done in shades of white and light blue. Whoopi Goldberg was the host of the event and it raised more than $1 million, making our first-ever fundraiser a huge success.

When I wasn't working on fundraising, I was putting the finishing touches on my second book, *Semi-Homemade Desserts*. It was a reflection of and testament to Grandma Lorraine's love for baking and cake decorating. I wanted to include all of her best recipes in the book. Each recipe had to be written so that the home baker would get the most elaborate, delicious results in the shortest period of time.

When putting this book together, I had remembered that one of Kimmy's and my favorite things to do in London was to visit the spectacular department store Harrods. Its famous food court takes up the entire bottom level of the store. There are small boutique shops inside the food court where you can find everything from caviar to cakes. The pastries are displayed in gorgeous dark wood-frame glass cases that light up from every direction, illuminating a dessert like a work of fine art. You would expect to see priceless jewelry displayed like this, but not pies, cookies, or chocolate.

I watched the bakers put their finishing touches on perfect petit fours using fine instruments and tools I'd never seen. As a child I used to love cake decorating with Grandma. She had the piping bags, nozzles, and tips to make perfect icing roses. I wasn't very good at it when I was younger, but I made great

171

little stars and leaves! It was an inexpensive way for Grandma to keep me happy and content for hours.

Harrods is where I was introduced to fondant icing. It was the icing that covered the most beautiful cakes I had ever seen. It's a rolled-out icing that can be applied over a baked cake, creating an extraordinarily smooth surface. It can be colored, shaped, and turned into almost anything you can imagine. I knew I wanted to put it in my dessert cookbook so I could share fondant with the whole world.

When I started writing the desserts cookbook, I went to Michael's craft store and JoAnn Fabric and Crafts. Both carried an entire section of cake decorating items, including everything from baking pans to icing tips. This is where I found Wilton's premade and packaged fondant icing. I couldn't have been more thrilled with my find because I knew this would make it easy for the homemaker to create beautiful cakes just like the ones I had seen at Harrods. The more I delved into the writing and designing of the desserts cookbook, the more excited I became. To me a great cake is a work of art.

Writing *Semi-Homemade Desserts* rejuvenated my passion for work. I planned out every detail and every photograph. I thought the finished book was glorious and something I could be most proud of.

During this time I was approached by Project Angel Food, an organization that helps feed men, women, and children who are homebound with severe illnesses. They asked me to get involved with their fundraising efforts as well as help build awareness in the Los Angeles community. They were trying to put together a special new food initiative to provide meal service for underprivileged kids who were going hungry.

Project Angel Food heard about the success of the UNICEF event and thought I might be interested in helping with a community-effort organization. Their timing was perfect because I was looking for a charity to donate all of the proceeds to from the sale of *Semi-Homemade Desserts*. Because this was a book created in honor of Grandma, it was only fitting that the money generated go toward community services. The book and the relationship with Project Angel Food came together quickly and easily. It was clearly meant to be and my absolute pleasure to partner.

In all my excitement, I called Mary Hart and shared with her the partnership with Project Angel Food. She believed in the cause so much, she immediately offered to write the introduction to *Semi-Homemade Desserts* as well as contribute any other support we might need.

Over the course of two short years, life had taken on a new direction that had meaning and purpose. I could use my power and place to help children have a better life. The prospect of that impact became my motivation to make Semi-Homemade successful so I could make a lasting contribution that could make the biggest difference in others' lives.

Chapter Seventeen
Partnering with Miramax

Life is about becoming more than we are.   *Oprah Winfrey*

In 2001, with two books now completed, and my passion for work reenergized, I had to find a publisher that would understand *Semi-Homemade*. All of my friends were willing to make proper introductions to the people who could lend a helping hand and give me a leg up to help me realize my dream.

One morning while discussing Project Angel Food with a colleague over breakfast at the Bel Air Hotel, I had an "Aha" moment. Everyone has an "Aha" moment in life—as Oprah Winfrey says, it's that instant when something just clicks in your head. One of mine came that morning when Oprah herself sat in the booth next to the one I was sitting in. She was alone and dressed in workout clothes. No makeup, no fuss, no frills, and no airs, just a regular person sitting down to have breakfast. She said hello as warmly as sunshine. I sat trying to grasp the concept of who was sitting across from me. The waiter stopped to take my order and I nearly recited everything on the menu. As he walked away Oprah turned to me and said, "Wow! That's a lot of food."

I told her that whenever I visited restaurants that had unique things on the menu, I order nearly everything to try new things and to rewrite the recipes for my books. Oprah shared with me her best store-bought secret for lasagna and to this day I can't remember whether she said it was from Costco or Sam's Club. At the time it didn't make any difference. Oprah was telling me who she thought had the best premade lasagna. I was thrilled to know that even she could appreciate well-made store-bought lasagna. It was validation in a moment—lightning in a bottle, received from the icon of icons.

Thrilled with my encounter and more cemented in my conviction, I knew I was on the right path. All it took was one magical moment of Oprah mirroring my message by sharing her own simple suggestion for lasagna. She made it OK for me, and nothing in the world was going to change my mind.

I shared my Oprah encounter with one of my girlfriends who suggested I speak with two powerful New York publishers, Judith Regan and Tina Brown. My friend's husband represented both and could easily set up the meetings with one phone call. When I initially tried to sell *Semi-Homemade Cooking*, these were the only two women I wasn't able to meet. I knew if I could only meet with them, they would understand the concept and how to help me best communicate the philosophy of my cooking technique. Neither was known to be a "cook," so I thought they would really embrace the overall message of the brand.

As long as I was going to be in New York, I took meetings with several other publishers too. Once again every editor I met with told me *Semi-Homemade* would never work because they believed you can't tell people what name brands to use. They insisted people wouldn't like being told what to buy and would reject the concept out of hand. It wasn't a book filled with healthy cooking tips, which was what was selling at the time. *Semi-Homemade* was dolled up down-home "mommy meals" and short-cut solution-based recipes. One publisher even told me the books made me look as if I were being paid or sponsored by the brand name manufacturers to tout their products, which I most certainly was not. These were hard-core New York publishers who believed cookbooks should focus only on made-from-scratch recipes. They didn't understand the daily pressures of the homemakers who didn't have the time or the money to spend all day in the kitchen but who still wanted to make special meals and a home for their families. Even though I believed in *Semi-Homemade*, I knew the publishers had already made up their minds.

The art of life isn't controlling what happens, which is impossible; it's using what happens.   *Gloria Steinem*

I was pretty discouraged by the response I had already received from the mainstream publishing world, so I wasn't counting on my last two meetings with Judith Regan and Tina Brown going well. Much to my delight, both women instantly got the concept and loved it. They saw the value in *Semi-Homemade* and how it could and would help. My first meeting was with Judith. She made me a modest offer on the spot that, after careful consideration, I decided to pass on.

My last meeting was with Tina Brown, who had just started *Talk* magazine and a new book publishing division for Miramax. Tina had previously been the editor in chief of *Tatler*, *The New Yorker*, and *Vanity Fair,* and had established herself as one of the most important women in publishing.

Celebrating Christmas, 1991, at Disneyland with Grandma Lorraine.

Making a cornice box window topper for the set of my infomercial, February 1992.

In the edit bay checking product shots and refining my infomercial.

Adding final touches to a bedroom before a photo shoot.

Filming Euro Kraft with Florence Henderson.

The finished window!

Creating a kitchen window treatment for filming, 1993.

The entire Kurtain Kraft production display at a Chicago trade show, 1993.

Below: the Growing Gardens product line.

Above: Shooting a gardening commercial with Cindy in Los Angeles, 1994.

In Santorini, Greece, on the phone with Linda from my office.

Me, Grandma, and Cindy at Cindy's wedding, 1993.

Me, my cousin Tracy, Aunt Peggy, and Cindy having dinner, 1994.

Johnny and me in Mexico.

Me and Kim: Baby time!

Grandma and me on our annual vacation together in Hawaii, 1995. She is wearing her favorite white shoes.

From left: Kimmy, me, Richie, Blakie, and Johnny at my nephew Brandon's football game.

With Danielle on vacation in Catalina Island, California.

With Danielle at Disneyland.

From left: Kimmy, Johnny, me, and Richie skiing in Whistler, Canada.

Lower row from left: Kimmy, Scottie, Brandon, and Danielle. Upper row from left: Lee, Michele, Richie, me, and Johnny night-snowmobiling.

From left: Austen, Brandon, Danielle, and Scottie jumping in the pool at Château Whistler.

Kimmy and me in Paris at the French Open tennis tournament.

In Tamarindo, Costa Rica, with the hotel's pet monkey.

With Dr. Ruth in Marrakesh, Morocco.

Looking at fabrics on a loom in Fez, Morocco.

Outside Sydney, Australia, feeding a wallaby.

My niece Stephanie and her mom, Kimmy.

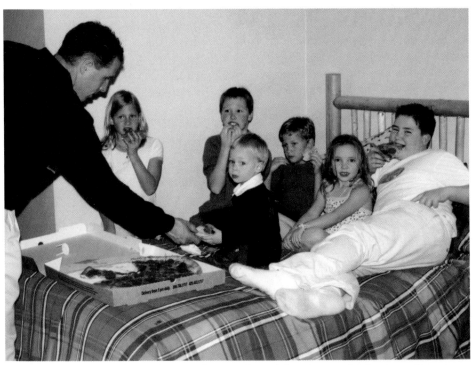

Richie, standing, with (from left) Danielle, Brandon, Blakie, Austen, Stephanie, and Scottie on New Year's Eve in Seattle.

Cindy, Kimmy, me, and Colleen at Tavern on the Green in Central Park in New York.

At dinner in Laguna Beach, California. Front row, from left: Danielle and Cindy. Back row, from left: Kimmy, Rich, Richie, Johnny, and me.

One of my last photos of Grandma, taken on our Alaskan cruise.

Shopping for the best ingredients.

In my kitchen at the shooting of the Semi-Homemade Desserts *cookbook.*

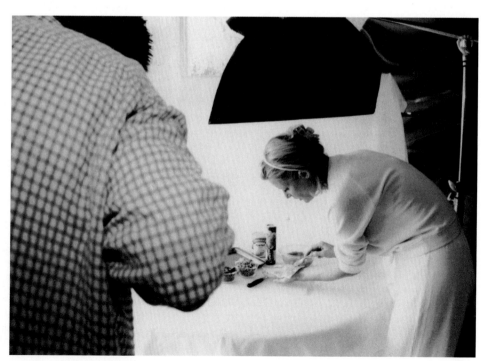

Styling a photograph of a dessert being shot in my kitchen for Semi-Homemade Desserts.

Me, Kimmy, and Stephanie discussing the Semi-Homemade *books.*

I wasn't sure my concept would speak to Tina, but I was hopeful she would think my ideas were valid. I had already proven the book would sell based on my success through QVC. Tina is a brilliant, savvy publisher, and I knew that if I could make her understand what *Semi-Homemade* could accomplish and how helpful it could be, that she would make it happen.

I made my best pitch to Tina. It was practically a plea. I thought the meeting had gone well, but you never know. I was on my way back to the hotel when my cell phone rang. It was Tina asking if I had time to meet with Harvey Weinstein, the president of Miramax. He and his wife were supposed to leave for the Hamptons, but he stayed to have lunch with me at the Regency Hotel. Tina said he had held his plane to see me and that I ought to be prepared to present a much bigger picture of what Semi-Homemade could become beyond publishing two books. As I rushed over to the hotel, I let my mind wander about all of the possibilities that Semi-Homemade could grow into.

The Regency is one of the places in New York where the most powerful men and women are known to meet to talk business. It was amazing for me, an ordinary girl from Wisconsin, to be meeting with Hollywood power player Harvey Weinstein for lunch. At the time I didn't know much about him except for his clout in the movie business from successes such as *Shakespeare in Love*, *Good Will Hunting*, and *Chocolat*.

Harvey was charming and sincere when he spoke. I told him about all of the areas I thought we could go into using the first two books as a platform. I told him about my days developing a television show with Dick Clark, about my product lines, about my idea for a magazine, and finally, about an entire series of cookbooks. All of these things would change the way busy homemakers manage their day. *Semi-Homemade* could turn an overextended existence into something pleasurable while creating more time for the important things in life—family and friends.

I explained to Harvey that my demographic was made up of women I call semi-homemakers who are between the ages of 35 and 54 and are generally running their households. A semi-homemaker probably has kids and goes to church. She is the new traditionalist. She plays host at the holidays and is the center for family and friends. She is a stay-at-home mom or a working woman. Of course, most of us know that all moms are working women. I know that most women in America don't want to do anything halfway for their families and my semi-homemaker is no exception. She's the one in charge, although she makes her husband believe that he is. That got a hearty chuckle out of Harvey.

In this day and age, a semi-homemaker believes she can be a superwoman—a combination of Samantha Stevens from *Bewitched* and Gloria Steinem. She can do everything with a twinkle in her eye and pep in her step. She wants to do everything quickly and efficiently so she can check off everything on her to-do list.

On the inside she's overwhelmed with pressure, but on the outside, she's too busy making everyone else happy to show it.

I could see Harvey soaking up every word. He could tell that I was passionate about the message and that I felt personally responsible for giving these women the tools and information to make their lives easier.

Harvey was moved and offered me a deal. He wanted to set up a co-venture between Miramax and Semi-Homemade.

I was elated that I had finally found partners who shared my vision and understood its purpose.

Before he would commit to signing a deal with me, he insisted I meet with his brother Bob. Shortly after my initial meeting with Harvey, I met with Bob at a restaurant in downtown New York City. Bob was charming and funny, but much quieter than Harvey. He listened intently as I recited the same overview of Semi-Homemade I had given Harvey, and then he asked for an example of a quick tip Semi-Homemade idea. The only thing I could think of fast was whipped topping. By that time in our meeting, we were eating ice cream for dessert. I explained to him the process of making whipped topping from scratch and the labor that goes into beating the heavy cream until you create light, fluffy peaks. Real whipped cream tastes like soft vanilla clouds. I told Bob anyone can achieve that result in seconds by using a container of Cool Whip and vanilla extract. Adding vanilla changes the original flavor, removing the packaged taste and giving it a refined homemade result.

Bob looked at me and asked if I was talking about the blue tub that sits in the refrigerator, the one you take out in the middle of the night and eat by the spoonfuls when you want a sweet treat. I told him it was one and the same. I went on to explain that Cool Whip could be used to make many other delicious treats by simply adding a flavored extract and a couple of drops of food coloring.

That meeting decided my future at Miramax. They were going to sign me to a contract. Tina was going to be my mentor. She made me feel free to express myself and to do what I thought was right. She encouraged me to present all of my ideas assuring me that if I presented a bad idea, fine, then it would be just a bad idea. But if it was a good idea, it could be our next best seller. If we were going to be in business together, it had to be collaborative in every way.

Let the negotiations begin.

Chapter Eighteen
I Do!

*The people who are crazy enough to change the world are the
ones who do.*

Apple Computer television ad

Creating a venture between Miramax and Semi-Homemade
was a long, complicated, and tedious process. There were
many moving parts because we were combining publishing,
television, and Internet businesses into one overall branding
initiative. Tina was remarkably supportive and conscientious
in guiding me through the negotiations, showing me that
Semi-Homemade was a priority to her and to Miramax. The
result was an equal partnership in every way.

During my negotiations with Miramax, Bruce and I decided
to get married. We set a date in October 2001. As I was busy
making wedding plans and finalizing the coventure contract
with Miramax, he presented me with a prenuptial agreement.
I had never thought about a contract for my marriage. To me
it wasn't a business. As I read through the document, my fairy
tale quickly became crushed by the act of one overzealous

attorney. He didn't know me and he certainly didn't know my relationship. I was shocked that my future husband made such a request and stunned by the aggressiveness of his attorney. I put up a fight for a while, but then I decided to give in and sign the agreement. I was secure in the relationship.

After my grandmother had passed, all of my emotion and my passion went into my relationship with Bruce. I hid in him and made him my haven. But something shifted with the swoop of my pen. After I signed that document, I no longer felt secure. I'm not sure if it was the act of signing the papers or the way it was handled that made me feel as though I were getting divorced and not married. I felt alone and unprotected.

Bruce was my love, my best friend, and my protector. Now he'd become an adversary. I was sad, angry, and disappointed. But I was assured by my newfound friends who had been through the same process that those feelings would diminish in time. I attributed the reason for my exaggerated emotions to the fact that I was simultaneously negotiating my deal with Miramax. On any given day one of those situations would have been tough and exhausting. On one hand I was going up against Harvey Weinstein, one of the most powerful men in entertainment. On the other, Bruce was one of the most powerful leaders in business. Both men were tough, strong, and excellent negotiators. I was left on my own to simultaneously negotiate against each of them. Together they were too much for me. I caved to Bruce and held strong with Harvey.

Just before our wedding and in the midst of my negotiations, we found a house in Bel Air, directly across the street from the Bel Air Hotel. The home had a rich Hollywood history. It was the original Greer Garson estate. Greer was an extraordinarily popular actress in the 1930s and '40s, and the grandeur of the home reflected her Hollywood success. At first I wasn't excited about the house because I was too overwhelmed by everything else that was going on. I wanted something small, quiet, and serene—a place that would feel like a true home.

As the wedding date grew closer and my stress level increased, purchasing a house was the least of my concerns. It was the house that Bruce wanted, so I gave in and agreed it was the right choice.

Several days after we signed the purchase agreement, the 9/11 terrorist attacks took place. We weren't sure if we wanted to keep the wedding as planned or postpone it. It had all been arranged. The invitations had been sent out and the RSVPs had come in. Despite that we pondered if it was right to celebrate a marriage at such a painful and difficult time for our country. We discussed it for several days with each other and trusted friends, all of whom encouraged us to keep the date as planned. Everyone agreed that we had to live our lives as normally as we could under the circumstances. As difficult as that decision was, we carried on.

Bruce and I got married on October 6, 2001, at Green Acres estate, one of the prettiest homes in all of Los Angeles.

Our wedding was an extravagant evening that I could only have dreamed of. Bruce spared no expense. I rented furniture to create a great Saint-Tropez midnight summer dream. I hired different bands to perform throughout the evening and surprised Bruce with a Neil Diamond impersonator—his favorite singer!

Nearly 250 guests helped us celebrate our nuptials. I found the perfect wedding dress on a trip to Paris, which I purchased off the rack for less than $800. I pinned silk roses into my hair and found beautiful pearls for my bridesmaids to wear. Everything about the wedding was frilly, romantic, and feminine.

My brothers walked me down the aisle, Cindy and Colleen stood as bridesmaids, and Kimmy was my maid of honor.

We were married on the upper lawn of the property on a beautiful fall night. We threw a great party. Everyone who was important to me in the world was there to share in my joy.

We had a jazz band by the pool, where a giant float sat on the water with 2,000 votive candles illuminating the cocktail party in golden amber light. There was an orchestra on the main lawn and a wonderful dance band at the dinner, which took place on the tennis court that had been tented and covered in lush carpeting. The table settings were burgundy and gold, a rich combination that stood strikingly against the soft lights in the room. I designed individual cakes for every guest to go with our grand eight-tier wedding cake.

After dinner the entire party shifted to an adjacent tent that looked like our favorite nightclub in Saint-Tropez. It was a beautiful and unforgettable evening and a wonderful way for Bruce and me to start the rest of our lives together.

We moved into our new home soon after the wedding. I had gone from planning our wedding to working full-time on our new house. The property was beautiful—an unimaginable dream. It had a creek running through the backyard that came from the Bel Air Hotel. The home and the yard had the bones of a masterpiece that just needed to be dressed in perfect design. Despite my initial hesitation I now felt fortunate for the opportunity to turn this English Tudor into the grand estate it once was.

Every house has its own distinct character, and like a family member, you have to be true to whatever that personality is. I designed the furnishings for the house so I could preserve its authenticity and charm. The first thing I did was decide on the flooring for each room. I laid out rugs to study the colors. Creating the initial framework always begins with the right selection of rugs and the perfect choice of window treatments. Those two elements instantly anchored my rooms and brought their personalities to life. Throughout the house, every room's framework was different and unique. Now, all I had to do was finish dressing them and add the detail they deserved.

Bruce surprised me with a trip to Rome, where we picked out incredible antiques. I couldn't wait to see our treasures placed in our new home. When they arrived and were set into place, I was thrilled with how warm, inviting, and comfortable the house had become.

My next project was the landscaping. In the front yard, I planted a rose garden alongside a vegetable and herb garden. I lined the entire property with small boxwood hedges, daffodils, and climbing ficus plants. I planted tall hedges that created a beautiful privacy wall on each side of the property. I covered the path along the creek in crushed brick that matched the house and planted ivy and asparagus fern from the top of the dirt bank, which cascaded down to the water. Climbing roses and ivy espalier covered everything else that had been left unfinished. They are the most beautiful way to hide any imperfections.

The house was finally complete. As I stood back and enjoyed the vision it had become, I smiled, knowing Greer Garson would have loved the result. Her home had been brought back to its original splendor. And it now had an owner who loved it as much as she had.

It's true. I loved that house. And for my first year of marriage, I put much my effort and energy into it.

Chapter Nineteen
More Bridges Than Gullies

Grief can take care of itself, but to get the full value of joy, you must have somebody to divide it with.

Mark Twain

Now that the house was done and Bruce was constantly working and traveling, it seemed like a good time for me to put energy back into my career.

So that's exactly what I did.

My goal was to develop Semi-Homemade as fast and furiously as I could, focusing all of my energy and passion on helping the semi-homemaker, who would appreciate the contribution in simplifying her life.

Just prior to the launch of *Semi-Homemade Cooking* in the fall of 2002, Harvey called me into his office to talk about publicity. He wanted to put the pedal to the metal on press and exposure. Harvey got on the phone and called in personal favors with such friends as Regis Philbin and Barbara Walters.

"Regis, have you ever heard of Sandra Lee? She is the new lifestyle goddess." Harvey spoke with such enthusiasm and excitement about our new venture that I couldn't believe my good fortune in having him as a partner.

The next call was to Barbara Walters. Listening to Harvey talk to Barbara about me was equally as flattering and completely surreal. Other calls were made just like those. By the end of our one-hour meeting, Harvey and team had secured a four-time commitment for me to appear on the *Today* show. I was sitting in a room with pure power and total clout and it was being lent to help support the launch of *Semi-Homemade*. I was in awe by the ease with which Harvey got all of these people on the phone. He wasn't reaching out to their producers, bookers, agents, or publicists. He was going straight to them.

While I was in New York, Harvey set up a lunch for me with Walter Anderson, the head of *Parade* magazine, at the Grill Room. Walter is a very tall, thin, distinguished, elegant man who is a highly respected journalist. I was honored to be invited. When I shared with Walter the Semi-Homemade philosophy and intent, he committed his support to helping in any way that he could. He was very kind, open, and thoughtful.

As we were lunching, Barbara Walters walked over to the table to say hello to Walter. My heart leaped with excitement. Walter introduced me to Barbara, who recognized my name from the call she had received from Harvey two days earlier. I happened to have the very first copy of *Semi-Homemade Cooking* with me that day. I handed it to Barbara, telling her it was the first off the press. She held it with both arms against her chest, promising she would read it that very night! She was gracious and lovely. I had planned to frame that first copy, but how could I resist smiling with sheer delight as I watched Barbara leave holding my book? What a moment!

A week and a half later, as I was walking from the Bel Air Hotel back to my house after breakfast, my cellular phone rang.

"Hello, Sandra? This is Barbara Walters."

These are moments I only dreamed of.

I stood alone on my street, dying to tell someone—anyone—I was on the phone with Barbara Walters!

There was no one to tell except the hotel gardener standing on the corner, who surely wouldn't care!

I had to remind myself to actually listen to the call. I was dancing for joy as Barbara apologized for taking so long to call me. She explained she had been in Cuba interviewing Fidel Castro. I was reduced to a giddy schoolgirl. Who could have ever imagined that someone would use the words Fidel Castro, Barbara Walters, and me in the same sentence?

Barbara invited me to be a guest on *The View*. She told me to come anytime. She said a producer would be in touch to work out the date. I thanked her for thinking of me as we said our goodbyes. I stood on the street outside my home and let out a scream. I called Kimmy and Colleen as fast as my fingers could dial the phone. That was a great day! Barbara Walters had called, and it wasn't a mistake!

A few weeks after receiving that call, I was booked to do a cooking segment on *The View* to officially launch my 10-city book tour for *Semi-Homemade Cooking*. On the day of my appearance, Whoopi Goldberg was the guest host along with *The View* regulars Meredith Vieira, Star Jones, and Joy Behar. Ironically Barbara Walters was not there on the day of my segment.

I was asked to demonstrate four recipes for four hosts in a four-minute segment. That gave me a minute a recipe, an impossible task. I knew it was important to communicate each recipe clearly or I'd never be invited back. The challenge was to get in all the information while still being fun and conversational and answering any questions that might be asked. Now if you've ever watched *The View*, you know it's sometimes hard to get a word in with that group because everybody has to talk and sometimes all at once! On that particular day, I can only describe my experience as a free-for-all, but it must have been entertaining because they invited me back several more times.

One of my next television appearances was on the *Today* show. It was their annual Halloween show, the highest rated show of the year. I dressed as Sandra Dee, appearing in a 1950s sock-hop dress with bobby socks and my hair pulled back in a ponytail. Matt Lauer and Al Roker were dressed as Siegfried and Roy. I couldn't help but notice that Matt's costume showed off his fabulously fit chest. Just before we went on the air I stopped Matt and said, "I know this is probably wrong, but I want to do something I'm sure I'll never have the chance to do again." Before he could respond, I placed my hand on his chest and said, "Oh my God!" He turned beet red and began laughing. It instantly broke the tension between us before we went on the air. We went on to have a great time during my cooking demonstration. I taught Matt to make a ghost cake from angel food cake and marshmallows, crunchy eyeballs from a box of doughnut holes and Lifesavers, and my secret witch's brew with soda pop and limeade.

That segment was a smashing success, so much so that my office received a call that would ultimately change my life. Unbeknownst to me, Kathleen Finch from the Food Network saw me on the *Today* show doing the Halloween segment.

Kathleen was the executive in charge of new show development and called me shortly after that appearance to offer me my own show. She said the network loved my energy and the Semi-Homemade approach to real home cooking.

I wasn't in my office when the call came in. I was on my way to a meeting at *Parade* magazine where I had been offered the opportunity to write my own column. I was very flattered by the network's enthusiasm, but wasn't sure I was interested. It felt too limiting for my new venture with Miramax.

Whether you believe you can do a thing or not, you are right.
Henry Ford

Sensing my hesitation the Food Network narrowed the focus of the show to just food, leaving me available to continue doing segments or shows outside that genre anywhere I chose. They entrusted me to develop any type of show I desired as long as it was based around food. The opportunity to bring Semi-Homemade to life on television was an absolute dream come true. Kathleen held my hand and walked me step-by-step through the process of creating the show *Semi-Homemade Cooking with Sandra Lee*. She made it her baby and enlisted all of the support of her colleagues, a team of powerful women who ran the Food Network, including Judy Girard, Brooke Johnson, and Eileen Opatut. These women have successfully made the Food Network what MTV was when I was growing up.

By Thanksgiving 2002 I received a call telling me that *Semi-Homemade Cooking* was number five on the *New York Times* best-seller list and the number one best-selling paperback on Amazon.com. Harvey sent me two dozen of the most beautiful white roses I had ever seen to congratulate me on the success of the book. I was thrilled to be making my partners happy. More importantly, I was elated that the Semi-Homemade philosophy was resonating with homemakers across America.

All of the touring and hard work was paying off.

Life couldn't have been better.

After the New Year, Semi-Homemade was in full swing. I was busier than ever, planning the television show, the launch of *Semi-Homemade Desserts*, and a single-issue magazine that Miramax had secured for me. All three were scheduled for release in October 2003. Bruce was also busier than ever running his company, and our schedules rarely seemed to match up.

Things were moving faster than I could ever have anticipated, and I was so grateful to have Tina guiding me. She had come to Los Angeles, where we were celebrating our great fortune and quick success when she received a call from Harvey to come back to New York. She took a red-eye that very night and was in his office by first thing the next morning.

I received a call from one of the staff members that same day informing me that Harvey was shutting down *Talk* magazine and Tina would be leaving the company. The flip, matter-of-fact way in which the information had been presented left me reeling. I was going to have to launch everything that had been set up on my own and without her guidance. I was shocked by the news and could only imagine how Tina must have felt. The venture had been going so well under Tina's direction. I called her to say how sorry and sad I was that we wouldn't be working side by side on all of the great things she had put into place. Tina assured me I would be fine on my own and that I had basically done it all myself. Her role was to guide me, and now, like a child leaving the nest, it was time for me to spread my wings and fly on my own.

After Tina left Miramax another woman took over her responsibilities. She had a much different personality from Tina's, which came across to many of our strategic partners as less than thoughtful of the brand. This woman was not a semi-homemaker nor did she appreciate the plight of the overextended homemaker who was the foundation of and the reason for the brand's existence. That message had been sewn through the fabric of all the relationships that Tina and her team worked so hard to put into place.

The new woman at Miramax was all business, corporate through and through, and she made me feel as if Semi-Homemade was an afterthought—an annoyance, as if it were just something else that had been put on her already busy plate. In addition, I believed her divisive actions forced a wedge between Harvey and me. My once flourishing and enjoyable relationship with Miramax was turning into quicksand. Without Tina it became nearly intolerable. There was no longer a big picture plan for *Semi-Homemade*. Everything that was once fluid was now confused.

Now on my own, I had to work harder than ever to maintain the vision that Tina, Harvey, and I had put into place. I felt as if I were barefoot climbing uphill in the snow—one step forward, two steps back.

By July 2003 I was preparing to launch the television show and create a special-interest magazine for Jack Kliger, the president of Hachette Filipacchi.

I was provided a small cubicle and desk in the *Woman's Day* offices in New York, where, unbeknownst to Jack, I was left completely on my own to figure out everything involved in creating the magazine. I had never done anything like this so it was a learning experience from day one.

The magazine was a holiday-theme issue, so I focused on organizing my editorial pages accordingly. I wanted the content in each section to be chockful of helpful information for my readers, including shopping pages with hints, holiday recipes, a complete party guide, and decorating ideas.

There were also many other elements to create, such as the table of contents, a letter to my readers, and an inspirational passage at the end of the issue. I was working on a shoestring budget, so I knew I would have to rely on pre-existing artwork and photos whenever possible. Thankfully I had kept organized archived folders of photographs from other projects I worked on, so there was no shortage of material for me to work with.

My managing editor was less than cooperative during the development process of my magazine. At a particular meeting, one of the editors actually flung her pencil across the table at me in total frustration with my inexperience. I later found out she had been at the company for years and was envious I was given the opportunity to walk right in and produce my own special-interest magazine without any prior time on the job. When she left the room I could hear her mutter under her breath, "Who's the new It girl from California?" Obviously my presence had ruffled some feathers.

Despite the resistance from other editors, I had to put my head down and keep my eyes on the prize. Jack reinforced this sentiment by often telling me the "prize" was a magazine that would help the reader better enjoy her holiday season.

So I did as Jack suggested and worked 24/7 over the next few weeks. With Jack's assistance I assembled a bare-bones team of talented art directors and editorial advisers to help me pull off the daunting task. I was responsible for setting up the photo shoots for the content of the magazine. This entailed finding new, affordable products in the decorating, cooking, and fashion areas. Each product needed to be "the hottest new thing" for the holiday season. My contacts with retail buyers were proving to be very helpful because they openly shared what items they'd be stocking on their shelves. I was sent more samples than I could have possibly used in one issue, but it allowed me to pick the best of the best, providing the reader the greatest selection of holiday gift ideas.

In the evenings after work and on the weekends, I would make the props that were going to be used in the various photographs for the magazine. I hot-glued rhinestones onto hatboxes I covered in white satin fabric to be used in the fashion shoot. I created red lollipop bouquets using a vase, Styrofoam, and shredded iridescent cellophane for kitchen shots. I strung garland made of gold beads and charms with white pearl accents for home design photos. Whatever props I couldn't make I bought from various wholesalers.

The magazine was coming together better than I could have imagined. My inexperience was a blessing in disguise because like the infomercial I had done years before, I didn't know that I couldn't do it, so I just did it! Ignorance was bliss. Once I went through this learning process, I gained valuable experience I could use in every area I was working in. It also helped me get even more in touch with the needs of the women I wanted to help.

One of the art directors working for the magazine found an amazing home location in Connecticut where we would be able to shoot the magazine cover and other editorial photos that still needed to be done.

The shoot was going exceptionally well. We were down to the three final set-up shots for the cover. It was a miserably hot August day—the kind of heat that makes you tired and lazy, especially when working on a set while trying to keep "holiday food" from melting under the extraordinarily hot lights.

Suddenly, in the late afternoon, all the power went out. We thought it was a temporary setback. But it turned out to be the largest blackout in the history of the United States. The entire eastern seaboard had no power.

Of course, because this occurred after 9/11, everyone was worried it might be another terrorist attack. No one knew what to think of the power outage or how it would affect the rest of our shoot.

My photographer received a cell phone call from her boy-friend, who was a New York City police officer. He insisted she get to their home in Philadelphia as soon as possible. She immediately began packing up all of her equipment.

"You can't go, we're not done," I said.

She shot back, "We have no power. There is no way we can still shoot a cover." And with that she got in her car and left.

The photographer's assistant stayed behind. I looked at him and asked, "Have you ever shot a cover before?"

"Nope," he answered.

"Well, you are going to tomorrow," I told him.

I needed to figure out a way to salvage the situation. I thought if we could just rent a few generators and find someone who had professional camera equipment, we could continue our work. I wouldn't allow the shoot to go over budget. This was definitely a time to prove what I was made of.

Wes, my food stylist, Kein, my prop stylist, the photographer's assistant, and I hopped into my car and drove directly to the liquor store. I walked in and bought the most expensive bottle of red wine they had. I didn't care what it cost. Desperate times called for desperate measures. I also purchased a couple cases of beer for the guys.

Adversity reveals and shapes character.   *Anonymous*

We gathered on the front porch of the bed-and-breakfast where we were staying and began to brainstorm whom we could call to finish the shoot. Someone handed me a phone book so I could scour the Yellow Pages for local wedding photographers and a place to rent generators. I thought someone would have the equipment we needed to finish the shoot. I used the last juice left on the battery of my cellular phone to track down a photographer, who agreed to work the job as an assistant to the assistant who was now shooting the covers. Wes and Kein were able to track down and order two generators so we could finish the job.

Everyone had a restless night due to nerves and stress. I tried to sleep with my windows open all night, but the buzzing mosquitoes kept me awake in the sweltering heat and humidity. I woke the next morning and sat straight up in bed as I realized that the shipping company would never be able to deliver the box of holiday ornaments I needed to decorate the Christmas tree for the cover shoot. The blackout had shut everything down. I jumped out of bed knowing I had to search the bed-and-breakfast to improvise. I asked the owner if she had any holiday ornaments we could use. Regrettably she said they were all packed away in storage.

I wasn't sure what I was going to do. I had no idea how to fix this. There was no time to make the ornaments, and no store carried any to purchase because it was August. As I opened a drawer in the kitchen to grab a spoon for my bowl of cereal, I saw the most beautiful heirloom silverware set I had ever laid eyes on. This was the solution! I could hang the silverware from the tree adorned with little red bows and they would be more special and meaningful than anything I could have purchased. Using silverware that had been handed down from generation to generation conveyed the importance of family and tradition. I nearly begged the owner to lend the silverware to me, promising her I wouldn't let a single piece out of my sight. As I hung them from the tree, I could never have imagined that something so simple could turn into something so sweet.

In the end all the equipment arrived and we were able to shoot three beautiful photographs, each of which could have been used for the cover. Our determination paid off. We all felt such a great sense of accomplishment, pride, and satisfaction.

As soon as that shoot wrapped, Kein, Wes, and I went directly to Millbrook, New York, to shoot the first episodes of the television show. The Food Network series was put on the fast track. It was only after I arrived on the set for the first day of shooting that I realized there was no script. Every word had to be organic and ad-libbed. It was just me in the kitchen with food and the cameras. If you're a fan of the show, you've seen that I sometimes have less than perfect days. I've dropped cakes out of baking pans and occasionally have had recipes not turn out the way they were planned. Even Julia Child has had to turn an omelet into scrambled eggs on live television!

The cocktail segment was never intended to become a regular part of the show. During my first week of filming, I decided to demonstrate one of my favorite cocktails, Jamaican Rum Punch. I had made the drink many times before so I felt absolutely comfortable with free-pouring the liquor without measuring the amount I was using. I was completely new to this type of television. I got caught up in keeping eye contact with the camera and forgot to monitor the amount of rum I poured into the pitcher. After I poured my concoction into a glass, I took a big gulp and got caught by the television camera looking as if I had just tasted gasoline. In fact, I looked straight into the camera and said, "That tastes just like jet fuel!" I laughed it off. What else could I do? As the old saying goes, "The show must go on!"

I think the spontaneity and uncertainty of the show is what gives it its charm. I have a team of culinary experts who prepare the food dishes ahead of time for the benefit of television, but I always create all of the recipes and menus, the themes, the decorating, and the tablescapes myself. My many travel experiences have inspired my tablescape themes. It was important to me to bring the creative and interesting designs I had seen from around the world to my viewers and present them in an attainable way. I use everyday household items or easy-to-find accessories that can be purchased at a crafts or home and garden store, making each tablescape easy to recreate.

The set decor also changes for every show to match the tablescape and theme. One show might have a crossword puzzle theme in black and white and the next show might feature a tea party theme in pink rosebuds. Every show is completely different and totally unique. My job is to share as many options with the viewers as I can. It's not about dictating what their tastes should be. It's about providing them with endless ideas of how to pull together the environment of their dreams.

When I started doing my television show, it took all day to shoot a single episode. Today, four years and seven seasons later, I can complete nearly three shows in a day. I learned to talk to the camera as if I was speaking to Kimmy or Colleen. I shared and explained my recipes and themes as if my best friends were standing in front of me instead of the cameras. It's a more intimate and conversational technique and one that allows me to just be myself. I knew I had so many things I could share, tricks I had learned, and tips that could cut any task in half. Although much of my knowledge had been born from my horrible childhood situation, I found a way to use those skills to make life easier and fulfilling for my viewers. The viewers are the real stars, the real heroes of the show.

Chapter Twenty
Eye of the Tiger

. . . I'm back on my feet, just a man and his will to survive . . .
I've got the eye of the tiger.

Survivor

Launching my television show made for a very busy life. It required me to be in New York more than Los Angeles, which meant significant time away from my husband. My communication with Bruce became very scattered because of the long days, the three-hour time difference between the coasts, and the terrible cellular service at the production house in Millbrook. Bruce was busy running his company and maintaining his nonstop travel schedule. He was a more mature, established businessman who was set in his ways. When we married I inherited a family and a lifestyle that was his. I was beginning to realize that marrying someone much older required me to make all of the scheduling sacrifices as well as be the one who was always flexible and accommodating. This is when I realized how hard it would be for me, his new young wife, to feel that I had equality in his already overcrowded life.

Our schedules never seemed to match up and I was no longer able to adjust my schedule to accommodate his. I made commitments to Hachette and had a contract with the Food Network that had to be fulfilled. Regardless of how lonely I was or how much I missed being at home, I risked losing *Semi-Homemade*. Additionally, if I didn't meet my contractual obligations, I could have been sued and all of the headway and hard work that had been done over the past years would have been lost.

Much to everyone's surprise the television show launched in October 2003 as one of the highest rated new shows in Food Network history. I received this good news back in Los Angeles while Mary Hart and I were planning a book party in honor of the release of *Semi-Homemade Desserts*. The party was planned in conjunction with Project Angel Food with Mary Hart and Eric McCormack, the star of *Will and Grace*, as the hosts. Eric was one of many celebrities who were gracious enough to contribute a recipe and lend their endorsement to the book. The party was held at the St. Regis Hotel in Century City. The turnout was overwhelming with nearly 300 friends and colleagues stopping by to help celebrate the publication of my second book and my new television show. My only disappointment that night was that Bruce, who had a previous engagement, wasn't able to come until the very end of the evening to help me celebrate.

Despite the great ratings of my show, *The New York Times* came out with a less than flattering review of both my show and my books. When I started in publishing, a publicist told me that I shouldn't try to get a paper such as *The New York Times* to understand my Semi-Homemade philosophy. She didn't think my methods were true to the culinary nature that the paper usually features in food articles and reviews.

Miramax hired an aggressive public relations firm to handle my brand. It was very difficult to find someone who truly understands food marketing, let alone a brand such as Semi-Homemade. In an effort to garner mass publicity, the publicist sent out a blanket press release along with galleys of both books to every newspaper, magazine, and television show touting the philosophy of Semi-Homemade. Of course she included *The New York Times* in her mailing, which culminated in their writing a scathing two-page review. I was petrified the negative press would paralyze sales of the book, diminish the ratings of the show, and destroy everything I had worked so hard for all those years.

To the credit of the Food Network, Kathleen Finch, the woman who brought me into the network, called me after the review came out to give me some inspiring advice. She told me that every time she reads negative reviews in *The New York Times* about one of their new shows or talent, it usually means that the person is going to be a big star and that the show is going to be a huge success. She wanted to assure me that the Food Network was 100 percent behind me. Kathleen didn't want me to get caught up or discouraged by this negative review. I was so relieved to get her warm and gracious call. And she was right. I had been genuinely worried that the fallout would be irreversible.

Thank goodness Kathleen took me by the hand to help me understand that this is the way things work in the food business. She was there to reassure me when I felt the brand was going to be in free fall after reading that article. Surprisingly *The New York Times* review actually had a reverse effect than the one I expected. It brought more attention to the brand and made the food industry and the critics contemplate their personal perspectives. Now they had to think through the philosophy of Semi-Homemade and the benefit to the homemaker.

You might have to fight a battle more than once to win it.
Margaret Thatcher

Semi-Homemade was catching fire with busy homemakers, giving me a platform and credibility in the business that no one else had. I was even asked to speak to the women in the MBA program at Harvard. I couldn't believe that Harvard wanted me to be their guest speaker. I didn't even have a college degree, yet there I was, sharing my secrets for success to the up-and-coming female business leaders of the country. It was flattering and humbling to be held in such high esteem by some of the brightest and most talented minds in the world. I was thrilled and moved by the experience.

The holiday issue of my magazine came out that fall. Peter Price, the president of the National Television Academy of Arts and Sciences, hosted a huge party at the Hudson Hotel in New York City to celebrate the successful debut. Mary Hart flew in to help celebrate and arrived with her dear friend Phyllis George. *New York Post* columnist Cindy Adams attended, as did Jack Kliger, Katie Couric, Harvey Weinstein, and even Tina Brown. I was thrilled to have Tina there with me to help celebrate all the things she had initiated for Semi-Homemade. It was her success as much as it was mine. Without her, Semi-Homemade might never have become a national brand. It was thrilling to watch my dream come to life through books, television, and a magazine. It was amazing to receive such great support from so many wonderful friends and colleagues. The only one missing was Bruce. He was busy that evening, and it was impossible for him to change his schedule.

Right after the publication of my second book, I received a phone call from representatives for the Cointreau family. They were holding their annual international Gourmand Awards dinner and ceremony in France and informed me that my first book, *Semi-Homemade Cooking*, was nominated for the "best easy recipes" award. I was thrilled with the invitation and delighted with the honor.

Finally Bruce and I were able to coordinate our schedules and we went to Paris. We met up with friends Jacques and Beatrice Ribourel and flew to the countryside. The ceremony took place in a huge old chateau. When I walked in, I was taken by the grandeur of every element. Each room was more sumptuously decorated than the last and every place you looked was filled with priceless antiques and magnificent tapestries. The draperies were extravagant and made of amazing quality. The chateau was illuminated by the roaring fires that came from beneath the handsome marble mantelpieces adorned by gold gilded mirrors. I am certain very few people in the room could have appreciated all the attention to detail. It instantly took my breath away and brought me back to the early days and my fond memories of creating Kurtain Kraft.

Much to my surprise, *Semi-Homemade Cooking* won the award. I couldn't believe my ears when they called my name to come up to the stage. I relished the moment to be honored as an international authority on the art of quick and easy cooking. I wasn't sure I would ever have the chance again, so I savored every moment.

Bruce and I went back to Paris. He had to work during the week, so I embarked on my own adventure in the City of Lights. I found a wonderful old store that specialized in cookbooks. I was amazed at how beautiful all the books were, especially those written by people I had just met at the ceremony a few days earlier. I bought two bags full of books to take back to the room and read. Even though I don't fluently speak or read French, I was still inspired by their gorgeous photos and layouts. I spent the rest of the week soaking up the beauty of those books, garnering whatever I could to use for my own ventures. It was a glorious time.

My husband was at a place in his life where he had earned the privilege to enjoy time traveling with his new wife. But I was no longer interested in our nonstop jet-set life. I began feeling frustrated by constantly being away from home and he was frustrated that I had changed.

I realized I no longer wanted that lifestyle when Bruce chartered a beautiful yacht for us on which we sailed around the Baltic Sea, exploring the Croatian coastline. I enjoyed the sun and the sea, but my heart was no longer into the carefree party lifestyle. When I could have been out shopping at expensive stores or having lunch at beautiful resorts, I found myself on the upper deck of the boat creating new ideas for my semi-homemakers. I felt more in tune with them than all of the luxury around me. I never felt completely comfortable in those surroundings or being so carefree when I knew that so many people struggle every day. And struggling was exactly what my marriage had begun to do.

When we got back to Los Angeles, I had to fly off to New York to shoot more shows for the Food Network. Due to the success of the show, they had decided to accelerate their contractual option for my next three seasons. I shot shows back-to-back for more than 12 months.

During this time my relationship with Miramax had dramatically changed. A friend who was an executive at Disney suggested to me that everything I was reading in the paper about the strained relationship between Miramax and Disney, a large investor in the company, was true. My friend thought that I should do whatever I could to take back possession of my company. He was very clear it would be in my best interest to salvage my brand before it was destroyed by the fallout that might come with the change in regime.

This news explained so many things I didn't understand since Tina's departure. The reaction I had been getting from the executives at Miramax wasn't about Semi-Homemade; it was about retaining control of their company. I had no interaction with Harvey for months. I don't think it came as any surprise when Miramax received my request to become the sole owner of Semi-Homemade.

Shortly thereafter Miramax gave me the price to buy back my company, all of the inventory, and the rights to the millions of dollars of contracts that had been put into place. The figure was astronomical.

I spent nearly the next nine months of my life going toe to toe, fighting with Harvey to make the deal. If I didn't come up with the money, my attorney told me that Harvey's plan was to liquidate the remaining inventory of books by dumping them at a dollar store to be sold for next to nothing. If that happened, it would surely ruin the brand and put Semi-Homemade out of business. The once kind and thoughtful business partner who sent me roses to celebrate our success was now threatening me with my biggest fear, losing my company, if I didn't pay his price. There was no room for negotiation. Though I endured massive legal bills that were large enough to buy a big house back in La Crosse, Wisconsin, I never gave up the fight.

The last conversation Harvey and I had was the day we made our final deal. It was a phone call between just the two of us. I was sitting in my family room at the house in Los Angeles when I decided to call Harvey. He immediately took the call. After a long, drawn-out, emotional conversation, we came to terms. Although it almost completely wiped out my personal savings, I bought back Miramax's rights to Semi-Homemade and was now free to do whatever I wanted.

As I was transitioning out of Miramax, Jack Griffin, a colleague at *Parade* magazine, called to say that he was leaving the company to become the head of book publishing at Meredith Corporation. He and I had a nice professional relationship, but we weren't close friends. When I heard about his new position, I sent seven dozen daffodils to congratulate him. These are the perfect choice when you're not sure what to send. They're cheery little heads of sunshine that always communicate best wishes.

Jack called to thank me for the flowers and catch up. He heard I was in the midst of buying back my company from Miramax and told me to call when I was in the clear. He said he'd love to publish my books. I was flattered and told him I would get in contact when the dust settled.

From left: Cindy, Richie, Kimmy, Johnny, and me in my living room.

Kimmy and me with Johnny and Richie on New Year's Eve.

Kissing Stephanie before getting into my wedding dress. My niece Danielle stands behind us smiling.

Me in my $800 wedding dress, zipping up Kimmy's dress on my wedding day.

From left: Colleen, Danielle, Cindy, and Aunt Peggy before the ceremony.

Uncle Bill and Aunt Peggy having a ball at the reception.

Danielle wants me to fix her hair while Stephanie prefers a professional stylist.

Johnny and Richie walk me up the leaf-covered aisle.

THE NEW YORK TIMES BOOK REVIEW

December 22, 2002

Advice, How-To and Miscellaneous

This Week	Hardcover	Weeks On List
1	**THE SOPRANOS FAMILY COOKBOOK,** by Allen Rucker. Recipes by Michele Scicolone. (HBO/Brad Grey/Warner, $29.95.) Preparing Neapolitan cuisine.	9
2	**THE POWER OF NOW,** by Eckhart Tolle. (New World Library, $22.95.) A guide to personal growth and spiritual enlightenment. (†)	2
3	**EVERYDAY GRACE,** by Marianne Williamson. (Riverhead, $19.95.) How the ups and downs of daily life can lead to an enrichment of the soul.	3
4	**GUINNESS WORLD RECORDS 2003.** (Guinness, $27.95.) A profusely illustrated collection of records about subjects as various as sports and technology.	10
5	**HALEY'S HINTS,** by Graham Haley and Rosemary Haley. (Haley/3H Productions, $24.95.) More household tips.	2

This Week	Paperback	Weeks On List
1	**DR. ATKINS' NEW DIET REVOLUTION,** by Robert C. Atkins. (Quill, $13.95; Avon, $7.99.) Ways to lose weight and achieve a healthy body. (†)	289
2	**THE WORLD ALMANAC AND BOOK OF FACTS 2003.** (World Almanac, $11.95.) The latest edition of a reference work issued annually since 1868.	5
3	**CHICKEN SOUP FOR THE SISTER'S SOUL,** compiled by Jack Canfield, Mark Victor Hansen et al. (Health Communications, $12.95.) Inspiration. (†)	6
4	**FIX-IT AND FORGET-IT COOKBOOK,** by Dawn J. Ranck and Phyllis Pellman Good. (Good Books, $13.95.) A collection of slow-cooker recipes.	17
5*	**SEMI-HOMEMADE COOKING,** by Sandra Lee. (Miramax/Hyperion, $19.95.) Recipes that are meant to be quick and easy.	1

The New York Times *best-seller list.*

The cover of the original Semi-Homemade *cookbook 2002.*

sandra lee
Semi-Homemade
Cooking

Quick Marvelous Meals and Nothing Is Made from Scratch
Introduction by Wolfgang Puck

Beatrice and me sitting on the plane on our way to the Gourmand Award ceremony in France.

I received the French Gourmand award—"Best Easy Recipes Book in the World." Beatrice was as excited as I was.

Mary Hart interviews Eric McCormack and me about Project Angel Food for the television show Entertainment Tonight.

Mary and me before the party starts.

Wolfgang Puck stopped by the party to surprise me.

Mary Hart & Eric McCormack
and
Miramax Books

Cordially invite you to celebrate the
publication of

SEMI-HOMEMADE DESSERTS

with author
Sandra Lee

an evening to benefit

Monday, September 29, 2003
6:00 p.m. – 8:00 p.m.

Hosted by

ST. REGIS
Hotel and Spa
Los Angeles

2055 Avenue of the Stars
Los Angeles, California

Please RSVP by September 19
response card enclosed

The invitation to the Semi-Homemade Desserts *launch party.*

Judith Light with me in the Project Angel Food kitchen preparing food and launching the new food delivery initiative.

The special holiday magazine, featuring the cover that was shot with borrowed equipment and rented generators.

The Christmas tree decorated with heirloom spoons borrowed from the kitchen of the bed-and-breakfast.

From left: Tina Brown, Katie Couric, Peter Price, me, Jack Kliger, and Harvey Weinstein at the party to celebrate my holiday magazine.

Phyllis George, me, and Mary Hart enjoy ourselves while talking to guests at the magazine party.

Shooting the "Daffodil Parade" episode of Semi-Homemade Cooking *on location in Sumner, Washington.*

Kristin, my producer; me; Jeff, my director; and Steve, my prop stylist, checking the camera angle at the tablescape.

Stephanie, Blakie, me, and Bryce in the car getting ready for the Daffodil Parade.

DAFFODIL
AMBASSADOR
SANDRA
LEE

Below: Me and Richie shooting the close of the Fair Show on the roller coaster, with Kimmy and Stephanie seated behind us.

Craig, my executive producer, discusses the script with me while the crew sets up at Northwest Trek in Washington.

With Stephanie at the opening of the Puyallup Fair.

The set of Semi-Homemade Cooking *on the Food Network changes color with every theme.*

The complete Semi-Homemade *cookbook series, as of fall 2007.*

From left: Mary Hart, me, Kaye Popofsky Kramer, Jane Kaczmarek, and Martha Nelson at the Step Up Awards, spring 2005.

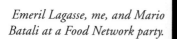

Emeril Lagasse, me, and Mario Batali at a Food Network party.

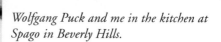

Wolfgang Puck and me in the kitchen at Spago in Beverly Hills.

Sammy's Chocolate Cake

1	box Betty Crocker® Dark Chocolate Cake with Pudding mix
1	box Betty Crocker® Fudge Brownie Mix
$3/4$	cup canola oil
5	eggs
$1/4$	cup creamy Red Birch Beer, Boylan's®
$1/4$	cup dark rum
1	can Betty Crocker® Creamy Deluxe® Ready-to-Spread Milk Chocolate Frosting
1	can Betty Crocker® Creamy Deluxe® Ready-to-Spread Dark Chocolate Frosting
1	teaspoon rum extract, divided

1. Preheat oven to 350 degrees. Lightly coat bottom only of a 9x13-inch cake pan with cooking spray; set aside.
2. In a large mixing bowl, combine cake mix, brownie mix, oil, eggs, beer, and rum. Beat with a hand mixer on medium speed for 2 minutes, scraping sides of bowl often.
3. Pour into prepared 9x13-pan and bake in preheated oven for 55 to 65 minutes or until tester inserted in middle of cake comes out clean. Cool in pan for 10 minutes, then invert onto cooling rack to cool completely.
4. In a small bowl combine milk chocolate frosting, dark chocolate frosting, and rum extract, and ice cake generously. Note: For a two-layer cake, you will need to double this recipe.

Sam and Alexandra out to dinner.

Me and Alexandra on our vacation in Saint-Tropez, France.

*With my friends John Hyland, Jeffrey Feigenheimer, and
the chef Raffaele Ronca at the Hamptons Wine and Food
Festival, summer 2006.*

With Katie at the Central Park Zoo.

*With Richie in Central Park in June 2007 during his visit to New York just as I began
writing this book.*

Enjoying Central Park, one of my favorite places in the world.

I saw the opportunity to continue developing the Semi-Homemade brand. I bought back all of the contracts that were outstanding and all the remaining book inventory and found my own distribution deal with Time Warner Books. I couldn't lose momentum. Incredibly, I recouped all of the money it cost me to buy back the company by selling the remaining books.

By October 2004 I was finally free to pursue another publishing deal. I called Jack and set up a meeting. Our publishing goals fit together like a dream. Jack and I signed a deal within a month.

When I was a little girl, Grandma Lorraine gave me a red-and-white-plaid jacket cookbook that remains one of my most prized possessions. The pages are worn, sticky, and covered in stains from overuse. The binding is broken, and the bright red color has faded, but the recipes still stand the test of time. Of course, I am talking about the *Better Homes and Gardens*® *New Cook Book* that was originally published in 1930.

I traveled to Des Moines, Iowa, to meet my new colleagues and tour Meredith's corporate offices. I was taken into the archives where all of the first editions of Meredith's books and magazines are kept. I slowly walked past a beautifully lit glass cabinet and saw the red plaid cookbook Grandma Lorraine gave me so many years ago. I was taken aback by my good fortune in partnering with Meredith. It made me feel as if I had come home to the family I never knew I had or missed. They allowed me to develop my ideas with full creative freedom and trusted my direction and knowledge from the start.

Meredith wanted to rerelease *Semi-Homemade Cooking* and *Semi-Homemade Desserts* and to publish a new book, *Semi-Homemade Cooking 2,* in the fall of 2005. I passionately set out to write.

Chapter Twenty-One
Closing the Door

It is the emotion which drives the intelligence forward in spite of obstacles.

Henri Bergson
The Two Sources of Morality and Religion

By Christmas 2004 my company was mine again and I had put a new publishing deal into place. I had filmed nearly all of the Food Network shows required in my contract, and I was exhausted to my core. The stress from all of the aggressive negotiations, the realization that my marriage was crumbling, and the pressure to sustain the pace of building Semi-Homemade had taken its toll. I was physically and emotionally wiped out. Although I was grateful for all the success, I desperately needed some time to reenergize.

Bruce and I took his whole family on a two-week ski vacation during which I slept almost every day while the rest of the family went skiing. When I wasn't sleeping I sat in the beautiful house we rented, staring out the windows at the snow. My exhaustion was turning into a deep depression. Bruce and I had drifted so far apart that I didn't even feel comfortable sharing my feelings with him anymore. I spent every day and night on the phone with Colleen and Kim trying to figure out why I felt so sad and alone. I was in a house full of people and had no one to talk to.

When everyone came back from skiing for the day, I pretended that everything was OK. I baked cookies while they watched movies. I listened to the daily adventures from the slopes, doing my best to be enthusiastic while putting on a happy face.

Although I loved being married, my relationship with Bruce had deteriorated. We were living two separate lives in what seemed like two separate worlds. During the months that followed that holiday vacation, I came to the realization that our marriage would never recover.

I spent that time analyzing my feelings and thinking about the implications of divorce. I tried to understand how something so seemingly perfect was no longer.

While I was going through these months of contemplation, one significantly meaningful event occurred that helped make my final decision about the fate of my marriage. I was being honored with an Inspiration Award by Step Up Women's Network, a nonprofit mentoring organization whose mission is to empower, strengthen, and provide community resources for disadvantaged girls at risk.

When I started to prepare my remarks, I realized that I didn't want to get up on stage and recite a meaningless thank-you. I wanted to say something that would move the room of donors to understand the importance of the work Step Up was doing and the difference their contributions made.

In preparing my speech I thought long and hard about all of the wonderful and inspirational mentors I had over the years and about what my life might have been like had it not been for them. I thought about the children in the room and what impact I could make by sharing my story. I didn't want those children to feel alone. They needed to understand that if I could do it, they could too. The message I hoped to convey was that anything is possible—all they had to do is dream big and work hard to achieve their goals.

I was very lucky to have Martha Nelson, editor in chief of *People* magazine, present the award to me. She had been the recipient of an Inspiration Award the year before and had come back to create a tradition in handing down the award from recipient to recipient. Mary Hart was also there as the host of the event along with special appearances by actress Jane Kaczmarek and one of the Step Up founders Kaye Popofsky Kramer. It was wonderful having such incredible women there to support me.

When I was introduced, I looked around at the sea of familiar faces I had seen so many times at social gatherings and other fundraisers. I knew my life story would change their perception of me forever. I didn't care. The girls at risk in the back of the room were now my focus. What I was about to say would hopefully open their eyes to all of their possibilities. In my heart I knew that I too, would never be the same.

It has been said that the best speeches are the ones that are kept to five minutes or less, but I spoke for a solid 20 minutes. There wasn't a peep from the audience. Near the end of my speech I had to look down to gather my composure. I had a lump in my throat and tears in my eyes and I could barely speak. The words were more painful than I could have ever imagined. When I looked back up, I saw my sister tightly holding hands with my friend Cari Klepper. I saw my friends, Alexandra and Sam, with eyes as big as saucers and Farideh and Ghada with tears streaming down their faces. I realized that there were many others in the room crying. I knew everyone understood how important their support and contribution could be. I made it more than clear when I wrapped up by saying we all had an obligation to make sure the girls in the back of the room would be allowed the same opportunities I had.

You cannot make yourself feel something you do not feel, but you can make yourself do right in spite of your feelings.
Pearl S. Buck

Bruce wasn't there that day, and now it was strikingly clear that he had not been there for me, the way I needed him, in quite a while. I immediately understood where our marriage truly was. I was fortunate enough to have many of my girl-friends there, and as I told my story, I could see each of them take in a journey they couldn't possibly have imagined.

After that day and for the next two months, I contemplated my expectations of a relationship. I loved Bruce very much, so I kept holding out, believing in my heart that things would get better, but nothing changed. We mutually agreed and I filed for divorce on May 10, 2005.

My years of living the jet-set life were fun but they weren't fulfilling. The perks and benefits were lovely, but all of the fabulous furs, fancy jewelry, and fun fetes simply weren't enough to fill my soul. A marriage isn't just a marriage; it's a partnership. You are destined to have good times and bad, but at the end of the day, I believe it is really about respect, loyalty, and being there no matter what.

They say that divorce is one of the most painful things a person can live through. I can tell you that this is absolutely true. One of the emotions that took me by surprise the most was the absolute shame in telling my family and friends. In my eyes, I had failed at one of the most important things in life. I had spent years building meaningful relationships and a strong foundation of family values with my brothers, sisters, nieces, and nephews. I always tried to demonstrate the importance of sticking it out through thick and thin. I never thought I'd get divorced. It simply wasn't an option, but now, that was exactly what I was doing.

I knew I had to break the news before anyone heard it secondhand. Bad news always travels fast. One by one I called my brothers and sisters and closest friends to break the news, but it took me nearly a year to tell my nieces and nephews. Mary Hart, Ghada Irani, and Farideh Bachmann were all there for me. That's what real friends do. When others go away they stay. They call you when times are bad to reassure you with their kind words and devotion. They go out of their way to ensure your success in things both big and small. They never let you feel alone, abandoned, or unimportant.

One of the most meaningful gestures of friendship came days after I filed for divorce. Ghada took me to breakfast to see how I was doing. She and I had worked very hard to launch UNICEF in Los Angeles. She lent a thoughtful and sympathetic ear, making me feel at ease and at peace for the first time in months.

Toward the end of breakfast, she presented me with a gift. I opened the box and saw the most beautiful ring.

Sensing my loss of words, Ghada gingerly looked at me and said, "Now you are married to your girlfriends."

That was exactly what I needed to hear at that moment in my life. Ghada stood by my side like the true friend she is. The ring was more meaningful to me than any possession I took from my marriage.

My dear friends Farideh and Thomas Bachmann insisted I join them on their upcoming trip to Turkey. They felt some time away to clear my head would do me good as I was very emotional. I thought it was a great idea because it gave me something to look forward to.

They flew over the week before I was supposed to join them. I stayed in Los Angeles a couple of extra days to tidy up some loose ends and to see my doctor because I wasn't feeling well. My appointment was on a Friday afternoon, which is never a good idea. In this case it turned out to be a horrible idea. When I described to him my symptoms, he gave me an internal ultrasound. Afterward he told me to get dressed and meet him in his office. I had been a patient of this doctor for more than 10 years. I had never seen him react like he did that day.

When I entered his office, he told me to take a seat. He very quietly and calmly began to explain that he was fearful that what he saw might be ovarian cancer. He reviewed my chart and reminded me that there were several cases of ovarian and uterine cancer in my family history. He wouldn't know more until he got my tests back from the lab and he wouldn't have those results until the following Tuesday. The doctor didn't want me to travel—there would be no trip to Turkey for me.

I was completely devastated and full of fear. I didn't want to call my brothers and sisters or anyone else for that matter.

There was no use worrying anyone until we knew for sure. Farideh was the exception. I had to call to explain why I would not be joining her and Thomas in Turkey. She was already there and immediately offered to come back so I wouldn't be alone, but I insisted she stay. I promised to call her the moment I had any news. Because it was Friday afternoon, I would have to wait the entire weekend for the results of the test. I spent those painful days all by myself, worrying and wondering, poring over the choices that I had made over the past few years.

The tests came back and, thankfully, I did not have cancer. I left the doctor's office and went straight to St. Monica's church. I prayed and thanked God for all of his generosity and for all the blessings that he has always given me.

It's very important to know that when you go through hard times, you are never alone. You have to regroup from the inside out. You have to be calm, reflective, introspective, thoughtful, and smart. You have to remember "Footprints in the Sand."

While I was waiting for my test results that weekend, I came across a letter I had received from Vicky in 1997. It had taken me six months just to open the envelope. When I finally did, I found an apology for the failings of a young mother so many years before, failings that she blamed on "ignorance."

"I know I didn't know how to be a good mother," Vicky wrote. "I'm sorry. Nobody ever taught me how."

She wrote of her own longings and how she wished she "could do it again. To do right by you. To give you the life you deserved."

And she finally acknowledged her awareness of Richard's behavior and her failure to defend me: "I never should have let what Richard did to you go unpunished," Vicky wrote.

"I should have had him punished and shown you, you didn't deserve that to happen to you. I was so wrong."

Vicky admitted many things in her letter, reminding me that she was very young when I was born, a fact that affected how she viewed our relationship during my childhood. "You were the glue that held us together," she wrote. "I thought of you as older than you really were and I wasn't mature enough to realize it."

She apologized for writing me a check that bounced. Her boyfriend had taken all the money from their accounts, she said. "I know it must have felt like a blow, but I really didn't have any idea."

By all indications, Vicky's letter was an attempt to extend an olive branch and make peace. "I never wanted to lose you," she wrote. "Please know I feel pain in my heart whenever I think about what I'm missing by not seeing you."

I had read Vicky's letter once and chosen not to respond. After reading it again and upon reflection, I believe much of what she said to be true. She was young and inexperienced and didn't possess the proper tools to be a good parent. I have spent a lot of time and have reached a point where I understand her illnesses, difficulties, and the circumstances she was faced with. I forgive her. As the Bible says, "Judge not lest you be judged."

I try not to judge others in my life—even now, my own mother. I feel the same toward Richard. I understand what happened although I know it is not healthy for me to continue those relationships. I know holding a grudge isn't healthy and that keeping all of that anger and bitterness inside would only transfer Vicky's toxicity into my life.

Reading Vicky's letter again that weekend was an epiphany because I suddenly realized what I had done. I understood why I was so sad and why it was incredibly hard for me to let go of my marriage. I was through pretending and no longer wanted to live my life to make someone else happy. I was an adult woman who had the ability to take charge of my life.

Get rid of all bitterness, rage and anger, brawling and slander, along with every form of malice.
Epiphany 4:31

Nothing is worth giving up your soul for. Money, fame, power, prestige—none of it is worth a dime if you aren't content. Your happiness, your true inner beauty, is not defined by your bank account or job title. You have to love yourself enough to know it's OK to not give up your very being for someone else.

There are no winners in divorce. In the end the prenuptial agreement that ended our marriage before it began turned into a blessing. It eliminated much heartache and pain. The divorce took just over six months to complete. Bruce and I were no longer husband and wife. We were able to manage the painful process with dignity and privacy, something we both agreed to honor and respect after the divorce became final.

Chapter Twenty-Two
You Can't Fake It

There's a whole other life waiting to be lived when . . . one day we're brave enough to talk with conviction of the heart.
Kenny Loggins

By January 2006 I was officially divorced and had moved out of our home in Bel Air. The thought of leaving the home I created and loved was heart-wrenching. The actual experience of moving was devastating. I spent months trying to decide where I should live. Staying in the home I shared with Bruce was going to be too painful. I didn't want to start a new life in a place that held so many memories from a marriage that no longer existed.

As I packed up my things, going from room to room I couldn't believe the last seven years of my life had been reduced to boxes and bubble wrap. The house felt empty even though it was still filled with all of the beautiful furnishings that I had found. I had placed every single thing in that home in its proper place. Going through the memories in my mind of how each and every piece of decor and detail had found its way into place was like saying goodbye to a family member.

This had been the home I loved, and I was completely taken by how emotional I felt. Until that moment I didn't have a clear understanding of what my own stable home had meant to me. There was no turning back. The documents had been signed, and the past had been sealed.

The hardest business call I had to make about my divorce was to Jack Griffin, my new partner at Meredith Corporation. I owed it to him to tell him I filed for divorce before he could read about it in the paper or hear about it secondhand. We had signed our agreement only months before I had decided to leave Bruce. I was working fast and furiously on the launch of our new book series. I was afraid that somehow my divorce would tarnish the brand's image. I would no longer be a "wife"; I'd be a "divorcée." I hadn't yet wrapped my own arms completely around what that meant or how that made me feel. But what I did know is that I had to give Jack the option to back out of the contract if he thought the divorce would negatively affect Meredith's business and put him in a compromising position because of his decision to partner.

Jack was very quiet at first. I could tell he wanted to be mindful of the big picture and the implications of everything I had shared. Then he confidently assured me that my marital status was inconsequential. As long as I maintained the strong quality of work and absolute brand conviction, he reaffirmed Meredith's commitment and partnership. He ended our call by cheering me on to get back to work. I was so relieved and felt positive that calling him was the right decision, grateful for his support and affirmation.

The day after I made that call, I moved to Santa Monica, the only other place in my life where I felt at home. I rented a warm, comfortable place overlooking the ocean. It was calm and peaceful, a place where I knew I could feel safe for the long months ahead.

Two women who had worked for me for years, Linda and Valerie, helped me settle into my new place. They were thoughtful and understanding as we worked over a weekend so we wouldn't interrupt our busy week of business ahead. Two days after I moved in, I had to go back to New York to tape another season of Food Network shows. I was looking forward to spending some quiet time with my friends Alexandra and Sam, who had just recently become engaged and bought a home in the country. Their home would be a wonderful, peaceful place for me to get away from the hustle and bustle of New York City.

The first day of shooting was tougher than I had thought possible. Smiling into the camera and sharing my quick tips to a happy life proved to be challenging. Even though it was eight o'clock in the morning, I asked if we could shoot the "cocktail time" segment first. Everyone on the set knew what I had been going through. I thought it would break the ice and get our new season under way in a positive and fun atmosphere. My humor instantly put everyone at ease. By the time we had wrapped, I felt stronger than I had in months and was so grateful that I had the show to look forward to every day.

We wrapped taping on a Friday afternoon. As soon as we were done, I hopped into my rented convertible and drove out to Alexandra and Sam's, where I spent the rest of the summer. In anticipation of my arrival, they had converted the upper level of their two-car garage into a small, cozy apartment. When I drove up the driveway I was greeted by Sam and Alexandra, who escorted me to my new summer home. We stood in front of the door. Before we walked in, Alexandra threw her hands in the air and asked, "Well, what do you think?" I told her I thought it looked adorable. I could hardly wait to see inside. Again she said, "What do you think?" That's when I noticed the most charming handcrafted wooden sign that said "Sandy Lane." I smiled and giggled because I could tell they had put so much love and attention into making me feel welcome.

My days and nights at Alexandra and Sam's were spent doing the simplest things. We'd go to the beach, shop in the local village, and have quiet dinners at home. For my birthday, Sam surprised me by baking a chocolate cake the Semi-Homemade way. He had heard my stories about the birthday cakes Grandma made for me as a child and wanted to make something special too. He smothered the cake in chocolate fudge icing. Alexandra's job was to keep me out of the kitchen for most of that day. The look on Sam's face when he presented his confectionery masterpiece to me was like a 6-year-old sharing his most prized possession with his best friend. The experience of pulling out three forks, diving in, and savoring every sweet mouthful . . . priceless.

Later that summer Alexandra and I went on vacation to Saint-Tropez. We both needed a break and the thought of beaches and dancing sounded wonderful. On the plane I read a letter that I had received from a woman whose daughter Katie had been diagnosed with leukemia. She was trying to put together a cookbook to raise money for a new children's initiative at the Children's Hospital of Philadelphia—Katie's Wish. She knew I sat on the board of directors of Childrens Hospital in Los Angeles and was hoping to gain the support of someone in the culinary world. She asked if I would donate a recipe for the book.

Upon returning from my trip, I called her to get more information about the status of the project and what other support I could provide. She shared with me that she had written similar letters to nearly every other Food Network talent but had yet to hear back from any of them. I could hear the gratitude in her voice that I responded and was willing to help her in any way that I could.

Whoever knocks persistently, ends by entering.
Ali, Philosopher

I offered her two recipes: one from me and the other from my 9-year-old niece, Stephanie, who was a semiregular on my show. I also offered to write the introduction to the book. Once I hung up I began to think about what it might feel like to have your child suffer from cancer. I had just gone through my own personal scare, so I knew what it meant for me, but I couldn't comprehend what it would be like to watch your child suffer like that. I wondered what else I could do to ensure the success of her project, as I knew only too well how hard it would be to produce this book. I also understood the importance of the work that Children's Hospital does.

One by one I called each of my Food Network family members—Emeril Lagasse, Bobby Flay, Rachael Ray, Paula Deen, Dave Lieberman, and Tyler Florence—to share with them Katie's story and the importance of this project. Every single one of them said yes before I could even finish. Each donated a recipe, lent their name and photo, and graciously offered any additional support Katie's mother might need.

I hung up happy and proud that my culinary family members stepped up. Next I placed a call to my colleague from

Parade magazine, Sheila Lukins, who is one of the most powerful and important women in culinary circles today. Sheila is famous for cowriting *The Silver Palate Cookbook* and her must-read articles in *Parade* Magazine. When her assistant answered the call, I could hear the hustle and bustle in the background. Sheila is a very busy woman whom I normally wouldn't want to interrupt but this was too important of a cause to not ask for her support. She immediately took the call and in a hurried tone said, "Hello." I knew I should make my plea short and sweet as she was clearly on a deadline. Sheila couldn't have said yes fast enough. Her recipe was in my email practically before we hung up.

Working on behalf of Katie's Wish gave me a purpose that summer. I could turn the anguish I felt while going through the process of divorce into a joyful energy by doing something positive for someone else. With everyone's support the proceeds from this cookbook could make a world of difference in the lives of the children and families such as the ones I had met while walking through the corridors of Childrens Hospital in Los Angeles. The experience of meeting those families and seeing those sick children has never left me. Once you've been touched by that type of experience, it's unimaginable to believe that anyone could choose not to help.

By the end of the summer, I was rested and ready to throw myself back into work full-time. I spent the next 14 months commuting between Los Angeles and New York, writing eight cookbooks, and shooting two seasons of the television show and numerous prime-time one-hour specials for the Food Network. Diving back into work helped me gain back my strength and helped get me through the rough times.

I spent Thanksgiving 2006 in Wisconsin with Colleen and her family. We took her kids to the Wisconsin Dells, an indoor water park, and caught up on life as we kicked back and watched her kids enjoy themselves on all the slides. We reminisced for hours about our college days and everything we both had been through over the years. Being with her and enjoying the simplicity of life in Wisconsin was the most relaxed holiday I had had in years. I left there feeling rejuvenated and with a newfound conviction for creating and living a more grounded life.

The stronger I got, the better I began to feel about myself, and my heart began to heal. Although the people who were my true friends remained my friends, there were many who disappeared from my life after I divorced. I started going out and making new friends. These friends accepted me for who I am, not for who I was previously married to. I was free to be me. I began to enjoy my independence and not fear it. I loved getting up in the morning and going for long walks in Central Park and along the beach in Santa Monica.

At first I found it strange not being married. I had no one to answer to, no one to clear my schedule with, and no one to tell me what I could or couldn't do. Eventually I came to like the way it made me feel. I was empowered by my freedom and by how far I had come.

I have found the older you get, the more of life's challenges you face, the easier it is to lose some of your buoyancy and resilience. It took an equal amount of time for me to feel as if I finally had my footing back as it did to get through those challenges. I felt strong again, like myself. For the first time in years, I didn't feel as if I were just going through the motions of life trying to get through it, but not really living. Now I had my stamina back.

I am certain that life takes you where you need to be exactly when you're supposed to be there. I understand that how we feel today may not be how we feel tomorrow. Life is all about perspective. I was dealt a hand that might have had a very different outcome if I ever allowed myself to feel like a victim.

I have learned that the only way to move forward is to live an authentic life and to be true to who you really are. When times get tough I always find that pulling back and removing myself from the situation allows me to gain valuable insights. When I was younger my silence was a way to escape my circumstances. It protected me when no one else would. It became a sole salvation in a painful and chaotic life. As I've matured I've come to understand that silence can be a good thing. Being still, quiet, reflective, and thoughtful is the best way to take one giant step back so that I can look at life with clarity and react with grace.

"Grace" has become one of my favorite words. To me it means learning to balance the good days with the bad. Grace is about being proud of yourself, your actions, your life, what you stand for, and the way you give back. It's being generous when someone hurts you; it's knowing when and how to react. It's knowing that someone you're not fond of today might turn out to be the only person who puts his or her hand out tomorrow just when you're about to step in front of a moving bus. Grace is offering understanding and acceptance when the rest of the world does not.

A woman with grace is the hero of her home. She makes everything happen for other people in her life but never forgets to make herself a priority too. She runs the household, where she is the strength and foundation. She teaches by example as much as she does with her words.

Everyone has the capacity to change. Your success or failure is predicated on your commitment to that change. The only mistake in making a mistake is not learning from it. Life has a funny way of reminding us of this every day. One day you're the toast of the town, the employee of the month, the leader in sales at your company, and by the next day someone else has taken your place in the spotlight. The ride up is never easier the second or third time around. We live in a world where I believe what goes around comes around. It is why you need to have grace. Life will always come full circle, sometimes when you least expect it. You never know who will reappear in your life or what situation will dictate the outcome of another. Resilience is key.

My secret to survival has been embracing life's challenges and not letting them dictate my frame of mind or determine my fate. There were so many occasions in my life when I didn't know what to do. Learning to stand strong in the face of challenge and adversity is the only way to get through the tough times.

Chapter Twenty-Three
From the Heart

If you have faith as small as a mustard seed, you can say to this mountain, "Move from here to there" and it will move. Nothing will be impossible for you.   Matthew 17:20

I think there has been a general misconception that I was born with a silver spoon in my mouth and was brought up with the power of privilege. I wasn't aware of this vast misunderstanding that had been presented through the television show and books until one day I received a call from Bob Tuschman, the head of programming at the Food Network, asking me to come to his office for a meeting. When I arrived he sat me down and shared with me that the network was producing a new series called *Chefography*. He said that Emeril Lagasse and Rachael Ray had already agreed to tell their stories. He asked me if I would consider doing a one-hour *Chefography* special that would feature my life story. I didn't know what to say because I knew that he had no idea what my background was. I wasn't sure that I was ready to tell the whole story or that he would find it appropriate given the carefree image we had communicated to the viewer.

The show *Semi-Homemade Cooking* was created to be a place where viewers could tune in to relax, forget about their own problems, find helpful information and sound solutions, and be entertained. I didn't want to bring anyone down with the weight that I carried in my heart. I looked Bob straight in the eye and told him the entire story. I needed him to understand the full impact of what he was asking me to do, allowing him the benefit of knowing all the information. When I finished, I sat back and looked at him. He clearly didn't know what to say to me. The first thing he said was, "I had no idea. I always thought your life had been perfect—that everything had been easy." He continued, "After hearing your story I want you to tell it now more than ever." He told me it could only help our home viewers. He assured me that my *Chefography* would inspire home viewers to know that no matter what they were going through, they had the power to create a happy home.

By the time I left his office, I had committed to do the show. Bob told me I had to start collecting all of the old family photos and archival videotape I might have. Doing this was more difficult than I had anticipated because I soon realized there weren't a lot of pictures that existed from the ages of 8 to 22. I did my best to pull together what I had and outlined the chronology for them.

We went into production right after Christmas 2006. I had no idea how strenuous sharing my story would be. The Step Up luncheon was the only time I had ever publicly shared the story of my childhood before—and that was a mere 20-minute event. And now I had to create an entire one-hour program. The first thing I did was call my brothers and sisters and ask for their permission to tell our story. I never felt the story was just mine to tell. I knew it would have an impact on all of our lives, including those of my nieces and nephews.

Welcome to your life, there's no turning back.
                                                    Tears for Fears

I procrastinated giving my interview as long as I possibly could. Everyone else who was to be a part of the program had told their stories and the time had come to finally share mine. By the time I got to my interview, I was more than raw. It had taken everything I had just to get through it. After the two months I spent pulling together the pieces of my life that I had so successfully scattered through my mind, compartmentalizing each and sending them out as if to the four corners of the earth, I had now brought everything back together and had to share it for the camera. During the interview Kimmy sat so I couldn't see her. We both knew that if I looked at her, I would burst into tears. As the first question came, I was overwhelmed. Tears began to well, and I found that I couldn't respond. Kimmy took charge immediately as if she were my older sister and pretended the director didn't exist. She helped me through the interview and I told the story of my life in sound bites that I could digest and clearly communicate. She instinctively knew how I would react to each question and, before the most difficult ones were asked, reminded me to breathe, nurturing me like the loving mother she had become to her children.

We wrapped production by Valentine's Day 2007. The show aired in early spring. It was one of the highest-viewed *Chefography* shows the Food Network had created.

After *Chefography* I thought enough of my story had been told and I was very happy to begin refiling everything back away in my mind—at least until I got a call from my publisher at Meredith, Doug Guendel, in the middle of May 2007. He knew there was much more to my story than had been presented in the one-hour special. He asked me if I had any interest in writing a memoir.

My reply was "A memoir? I'm 40 years old! Aren't you supposed to wait until you're at least 60?"

He used a similar argument to the one he used when he convinced me to write the "slow cooker" series of cookbooks. He said, "It's about what's useful to the semi-homemaker." He wanted me to understand that if I could get to this stage in life after all the challenges I had to overcome, certainly no matter where my home heroes were in their lives, I could assure them that they could reach their goals too.

I asked Doug when he'd want to release the book if I'd agree to do it. He said, "November."

"Of this year?" I replied.

He said yes and told me my biggest challenge would be that I only had six weeks to write it. Writing a memoir can sometimes take years to write. Even so, I agreed to do it unaware of how painful it would be to once again relive each and every stage of my life. There were days when I wrote that I had no idea how hurt I was still. Halfway through the book, right after I finished the chapter where I laid Grandma to rest, I went to bed for two days and cried. I was sick to my stomach and heartbroken all over again. I thought about walking away from the project. I called my editor at Meredith and told him I was struggling. I broke down in tears as he patiently listened. When I finished telling him how I felt, he told me it would be OK if I decided not to finish, that the company would understand. But he also reminded me that there are many people who would read this book who are currently in places I had been. I had the power and knowledge to help them in ways that I never had before.

I spent the following two days that I should have been writing, thinking. At the time my brother Richie was visiting me in New York. He and I went for walks in Central Park and talked for hours about our individual childhood memories and experiences.

He thought that I should tell my story. With the encouragement of my editor and several other trusted friends and advisers along with the blessing of my other siblings, I was persuaded to carry on. As difficult as it might be, my heart told me I had an obligation to finish the book. If my story could make a difference in one person's life, then it would all be worth it.

I have always been lucky to meet strong women and men who have been very thoughtful and helpful, even gently pushing me in the right direction along the way. I'm not sure they ever knew what a gift they gave me in sharing their knowledge and expertise. But I will forever be grateful for their time and commitment to helping me succeed.

Carole Black, a girlfriend of mine, gave me a special paperweight for my birthday a few years back that reads, "What would you attempt to do if you knew you could not fail?"

I use that phrase as often as possible because it inspires me to live a limitless life. Carole is one of those wonderfully strong and fearless women. The paperweight sits on my desk to remind me that fear is the only thing that can hold us back. Someone once told me that FEAR is an acronym for False Evidence Appearing Real. Once I grasped that concept, especially while writing my memoir, I never looked back.

As I began the process of writing this memoir, I attended a party in honor of Tina Brown's new book, *The Diana Chronicles*. I knew she had been consumed with the research and writing of it for several years and was thrilled to be able to celebrate her most recent accomplishment and success. Tina's book was the talk of New York and everywhere else, and, although I was overjoyed for her, I felt excited and nervous when I walked into the room because this would be the first time I would see many of the familiar faces from the time I was married to Bruce, as well as the original team from Miramax. I wasn't sure what to expect or exactly who would be there, but I knew the most powerful people in New York would be among the many guests. The party took place in the private club on top of the Sony headquarters in New York. The room was flooded with light from the many floor-to-ceiling windows that surround the space.

I was touched by the warm greetings I received from several of the people there who genuinely communicated how much they'd missed seeing me. I was equally surprised at how happy I was to see them too. After wishing Tina well and chatting with other friends I had made over the years who were in the room, the party was coming to an end. As I walked toward the door to leave, I spotted Harvey Weinstein walking in. I couldn't believe he was there after everything that had happened between Tina and him. I wasn't sure how I would feel about seeing him for the first time since we'd ended our business relationship. Much to my surprise, it felt good. He looked terrific. He was beaming as he walked up to me and gave me a peck on the cheek. He was his charming and delightful self. We chatted for only a minute before I wished him well and was on my way. What Tina and Harvey taught me that evening was that sometimes there is an opportunity for growth and closure in the simplest gestures and experiences.

Attending that party made me realize that I could be out there again in the social scene, but this time all on my own. I didn't need Bruce to fit in and feel safe. I felt good about where I was in my life. I practically hid away from socializing with the jet set for nearly 18 months after my divorce. Tina Brown had opened the door to New York when she offered me my deal at Miramax, and now, without her knowing it, she had done the same thing again by including me in her celebration.

It's taken me years, but I have finally gotten to a place where I feel content and comfortable with my own value and unique contribution. I have consistency and security in my life. And, although I don't have any children of my own, it's important to know that I consider my brothers, sisters, nieces, and nephews my children. I feel as if I have had kids since I was 7 years old. I have spent my life helping and protecting them like a proud parent. I feel fulfilled and satisfied in my relationships with each of them. I'm not sure I could feel more love or be more content even if I had given birth to them myself. They each give me so much joy and pleasure.

Although I don't maintain a relationship with Richard, Kimmy and my brothers do. He is still married to Gloria, who, in retrospect, I now understand helped me keep in touch with my brothers and sisters after I moved to Wisconsin. I have great admiration for her and gratitude for all of her selflessness on behalf of our family.

My brothers and my sister Kimmy still live in Washington.

Richie has grown into an incredible man. He married Michele, his high school sweetheart, and they have been together for 16 years. They have three beautiful kids, Brandon, Blake, and Katie.

Kimmy is married to Lee, whom she has also known since high school. They have three children, Scottie, Stephanie, and Bryce.

Johnny, my youngest brother, lives down the street from Richie with his two dogs. He plays baseball and travels often to play in tournaments.

Cindy still lives in Arizona, not far from where Grandma Lorraine lived. She's a single mom and has three children, Danielle, Austen, and Taner. She works in building and land development.

I love being Aunt Sandy to all of my nieces and nephews. I spend as much time with them as possible. They often come to see me in California or New York. My nieces have grown into what we playfully refer to as "Sandra Lee girls." Sandra Lee girls don't wear short skirts, don't cuss, and are always kind and graceful. Sandra Lee girls strive to be the best they can be. They get good grades, they travel, and they won't be getting married until they are at least 40! It's something of a running joke in our family, but it does inspire my nieces in a positive way. I try to set an example for the girls like Grandma set for me.

My siblings and I speak nearly every day. We see each other as many times as possible during each year, usually when I find myself in Seattle for business. Each of them comes to New York to shoot the show and for weekend visits.

I am extremely proud of how my family has turned out. Everyone is happy, healthy, and living a good life. None of us feels like a victim of our circumstances from growing up. We have taken the lemons life has handed us and made sweet, delicious, homemade lemonade. We are all blessed to have remained close, even when life is hard. Looking back, I would have wished for an easier, more stable life for all of us, but I have to believe that our upbringing and struggles have made us stronger. I'll never really know if life would have been better if things had been different. All I can do is thank God every day that we have one another.

If I had to live my life again, I'd make the same mistakes, only sooner.   *Tallulah Bankhead*

Many times in life I have looked up at the sky and said aloud, "*Why* do I have to go through this?" It's clear to me now that everything has a reason and a purpose. Our job is to figure out what lesson we're supposed to learn from each experience and how to use it in our own lives or impart it to others. Every day I become clearer and clearer about what's right and what a gift, not a curse, my childhood was.

There's an art to living a good life. Life is what you make of it. We are all responsible for ourselves, our success, and our failures. Picking up and moving forward is the only thing we can do. And making your life matter is the most important thing.

I didn't need to write this book to make a living. I did it to help others make a life. I want to inspire others who might be discouraged by difficulty. We all live life in stages. All we can do is strive to live those stages the best we can. Every life has pain and vulnerability. As beautiful as my life may appear on TV, as if it's all roses and cupcakes, I have bad days too—just like you. In fact there are weeks that seem to have more bad days than good. I have learned you have to put yourself first and then lift up your family and friends as you go. Be as smart as possible with the information you have and practice the lessons you've learned along the way.

It took a lot of soul-searching to share my story with you. I wasn't confident that I had experienced enough life yet to make this book meaningful or helpful. And yet now that I have gone through the process of recalling the ups and downs, the triumphs and tragedies, the tears and the joy, I realize that the true path to self-discovery is sharing your truth with others so they can benefit from lessons learned and experience gained through the trials and tribulations of growing up.

I hope that my story has inspired you in your own life and that you are able to take away nuggets of hope to help you get through any of life's challenges. I've learned we can all have success, a little glamour, and excitement in our lives, but it must truly be authentic. I am still a work in progress but know in my heart that I am well on my way to being completely happy and whole in a life that was truly made from scratch.

WITH APPRECIATION

To Laura Morton, for getting me through the tears and the heartache, for helping me bring my memories to life, and working so passionately to make them meaningful. You have been my "Footprints in the Sand."

To Jack, Doug, Peggy, Linda, Rich, Gayle, Stacy, Martha, Lee, and Lisa for supporting and advising me.

To John and Mario for your enthusiasm, help, and guidance.

To my editorial team Adam, Alrica, Greg, Jan, Jane, Jerry, Karla, Ken, Larry, Matt, Mick, Peter, and Rob. Thank you for your commitment and help in making this project come together in record time! I couldn't have done it without you.

WITH LOVE AND GRATITUDE

To Cindy, Kimmy, Richie, and Johnny, for a life of love and friendship and the gifts of your children. For your commitment in keeping us all together and mostly for just being your wonderful selves. Thank you for allowing me to write this book and for understanding that if it helps just one person it will have been worth it. I love you with all my heart.

Always and forever. SL

To Aunt Peggy and Uncle Bill for always being there for us.

To Colleen, the best friend in the world. I know it is cliche, but you'll always be the wind beneath my wings!

To Sam and Alexandra, for everything. No words could express how lucky I was to meet you. Thank you for all your help.

To Andrew, Mariah, Cara, and Michaela, for keeping me focused and for bringing me such joy.

To Farideh, Ghada, Judith, Mary, and Tina for your friendship, love, and support.

Most of all, thank you to Grandma Lorraine.